The

FORGOTTEN
FOUNDATIONS

of

FUNDRAISING

The

FORGOTTEN
FOUNDATIONS

of

FUNDRAISING

Practical Advice and Contrarian Wisdom
for Nonprofit Leaders

JEREMY BEER | JEFFREY CAIN

WILEY

For general information on our other products and services or for technical support, please contact our Customer Care Department within the United States at (800) 762-2974, outside the United States at (317) 572-3993 or fax (317) 572-4002.

Wiley publishes in a variety of print and electronic formats and by print-on-demand. Some material included with standard print versions of this book may not be included in e-books or in print-on-demand. If this book refers to media such as a CD or DVD that is not included in the version you purchased, you may download this material at http:// booksupport.wiley.com. For more information about Wiley products, visit www.wiley .com.

Library of Congress Cataloging-in-Publication Data

Names: Beer, Jeremy, 1972– author. | Cain, Jeffrey J., 1965– author.
Title: The forgotten foundations of fundraising : practical advice and
   contrarian wisdom for nonprofit leaders / Jeremy Beer and Jeff Cain.
Description: Hoboken, New Jersey : John Wiley & Sons, Inc., [2019] | Includes
   index. |
Identifiers: LCCN 2018054063 (print) | LCCN 2018057397 (ebook) | ISBN
   9781119546450 (AdobePDF) | ISBN 9781119546474 (ePub) | ISBN 9781119546467
   (hardcover)
Subjects: LCSH: Fund raising. | Nonprofit organizations—Management.
Classification: LCC HV41.2 (ebook) | LCC HV41.2 .B44 2019 (print) | DDC
   658.15/224—dc23
LC record available at https://lccn.loc.gov/2018054063

Cover Design: Wiley
Cover Image: © xefstock/iStock.com

Printed in the United States of America

V10008078_020619

*To all our colleagues and clients, past and present,
for helping strengthen the little platoons.*

Contents

The
FORGOTTEN
FOUNDATIONS
of
FUNDRAISING

Chapter 1

Civil Society, Yes; Sheepskins on the Wall, No—or, the Cons of Being Pro

This is a book for people who hate these kinds of books. This book is also an act of reclamation. We aim to take back fundraising from the professionals and the degreed class, with their impenetrable jargon and their fetishized algorithms and their extortionate fees, and return it to its proper owners: Catholic-school moms, CEOs of smaller nonprofits, symphony orchestra development officers, idealistic think-tankers . . . the people who are the heart and soul of American civil society. Because civil society is not an exclusive club; it's a participatory democracy. It is citizenship in glorious action.

We don't like to bask in self-adulation, at least no more than any relatively normal person does. We don't like to toot our own horns, write our own press releases, or pen advertisements for ourselves. We don't want to come off as what sixth-grade girls used to call "conceited."

But, oh heck, let's.

Nah, we won't, but we do need to give you a brief and unadorned corporate resume in anticipatory response to a reader's inevitable question: "Just who are these guys, and why should I listen to them?"

We are Jeremy Beer and Jeff Cain. In 2009, we founded American Philanthropic, a consultancy that shuns secret formulas and magic bullets. Instead, AmPhil provides empirically based strategic guidance, essential tools, and practical training. Though the authors hold doctorates in Psychology and English Literature, respectively, please don't hold that against us: This book is academese-free, and not once will we use the words *instantiate* or *semiotics*.

Though our two names are blazoned on the cover, this really is a collaborative effort by all 30 or so of us at American Philanthropic, where Jeremy is now Principal Partner while Jeff toils as the CEO of CrossFit. Also pitching in for this effort was our friend Bill Kauffman, who is neither cross nor fit.

We and our colleagues have worked with hundreds of nonprofits over the last decade and helped them raise more than oodles but fewer than gazillions of dollars—we won't insult your intelligence by hanging a precise number on it, the way many consultants do. We learned much of what follows from our clients. And we learned by trial and error, by instinct and empiricism, by following promising leads down dead-end roads and stumbling into unexpected revelations. Our intention is to jump the reader 10 years ahead of where we were when we launched American Philanthropic.

Simplify, simplify, simplify is a simplistic mantra, but if you do two things well, you will raise ample funds: (1) Find new donors, and (2) cultivate the donors you have, moving them up the giving ladder. That's it.

Well, it's a little more complicated than that. Likewise, you could say that offensive football consists of just two things—running and passing the ball—but success depends upon how well you execute a variety of plays, formations, and strategies. In the case of fundraising, your playbook primarily consists of direct mail, meetings, and foundation grants. Down, set, *hut*. Perform these well and you'll raise more than enough money.

Fundraising isn't rocket science; in fact, the asocial father of rocket science, Robert Goddard, who was often distracted and unpleasant, would have been a lousy fundraiser, though the charismatic Werner von Braun might have done just fine if the space flight thing didn't work out for him.

What the world of fundraising *is*, though, is a banquet for those who feast on bad ideas.

In the early years of the company, we were continually surprised at our success. At first we thought that we were getting away with something, pulling the wool over our clients' eyes. After all, we had modest experience in fundraising and, at some level, felt that we were not qualified to teach others. We did in fact have a lot to learn. Over the years, though, and with the help of our wise clients and superb colleagues, we have found a way of doing things that works. We're still learning on the fly; anyone who has stopped learning has started to atrophy, and the next stop is complacent mediocrity. But we now understand more completely where we stand in the bigger scheme of fundraising professionals and nonprofit consulting companies. To borrow a lyric from those puckish nonconformists of the first wave of British rock, the Kinks, we're not like everybody else.

Some of the conventional wisdom about fundraising is, we have found, self-serving nonsense spooned out by consultants who benefit from its tenets. When we launched American Philanthropic, we had no reason or incentive to dissent from this conventional wisdom. Its bland certitudes seemed unobjectionable, if uninspiring.

But the realities of guiding hundreds of small and medium nonprofits toward fiscal health jolted us into the realization that the bland certitudes of the conventional wisdom are based on gross misunderstandings of human nature and why people give money to nonprofits. In obsessing over numbers, outcomes, and its endlessly advertised "rationalism," the fundraising establishment has often excluded the human factor from its calculations.

To the extent American Philanthropic has been successful, it is in part because we operate under no grand theory, no peremptory ideology. We take a simple nuts-and-bolts approach that we call, jokingly, DIRT. (Every scam artist and grifter who carries a business card identifying himself as a consultant traffics in acronyms; we chose ours with tongue only partly in cheek, since dirt is, quite literally, down to earth, and that's where we operate.)

We will dig into DIRT in the second chapter. For now, let's just point out that DIRT is what feeds the grassroots, and this humble agrarian metaphor fits the American Philanthropic philosophy. We stand, first and last, for civil society and for the idea that ordinary Americans—working in concert and motivated by love and fellowship and strong conviction within the private associations, societies, and charitable organizations that give America its pith, its heart, its spirit—are more valuable than the entire run of top-down, heavily credentialed, remote-controlled nonprofit Godzillas.

Don't be cowed by the arcane—often inane—language of the professional fundraiser. You don't need a degree in fundraising or a certificate in philanthropy, although several of our best friends in the field are so credentialed. "Let every sheep keep its own skin,"[1] as Henry David Thoreau famously dismissed the acquisition of diplomas. Given that both of AmPhil's founders possess a PhD, we are not in full accord with the Thoreauvian sentiment, but we appreciate its implicit endorsement of native common sense and American autodidacticism over pedantic displays of formal learning.

If you are reasonably bright and interpersonally normal, you already have the necessary skills to raise money for your nonprofit. We'll give you the tools and tell you what you need to know. Follow our advice—get down in the DIRT—and you'll be successful. You'll also save yourself a lot of grief, not to mention money. (Doctorates in philanthropy don't come cheap!)

In the chapters that follow, we'll tell you how to find donors and how to keep them, how to plan for organizational success and how to achieve it, and how best to employ mailings, meetings, events, donor clubs, planned giving, foundation outreach, and more in furtherance of your nonprofit's goals.

We mentioned *civil society*, which has about it the whiff of a buzzword, an empty vocable of the sort used by hack political speechwriters.

It's not. Civil society is just a faintly pretentious name for America. For the essence of America is voluntary human collaboration and mutual aid. It is community, sodality, solidarity, pursued collectively but noncoercively.

Civil society is what makes America *America*. It is the Little League, the volunteer fire department, the quilting guild, the historical society, the Society of St. Vincent de Paul and the deacons of the Presbyterian Church and the African Methodist Episcopal Church choir and the Candy Stripers and the town's concert band and the reggae circle and the Gilbert & Sullivan amateur troupe and the Village Green Preservation Society. And sure, a rung or two up the ladder it also includes your city's aquarium, museums, liberal arts college, and other well-heeled institutions.

Though diminished, service clubs remain the civic backbone of many communities: Rotary, Lions, Kiwanis, Zonta, Elks. They are part of the American legacy of voluntary associations. They undergird our communities; without them, we may as well be free-floating atoms, unconnected and wanton.

Alexis de Tocqueville, the keen-eyed French observer of the American scene during the Jacksonian era, marveled at the profusion of voluntary associations within the new republic:

Americans of all ages, all conditions, and all dispositions constantly form associations. They have not only commercial and manufacturing companies, in which all take part, but associations of a thousand other kinds, religious, moral, serious, futile, general or restricted, enormous or diminutive. The Americans make associations to give entertainments, to found seminaries, to build inns, to construct churches, to diffuse books, to send missionaries to the antipodes; in this manner they found hospitals, prisons, and schools. If it is proposed to inculcate some truth or to foster some feeling by the encouragement of a great example, they form a society. Wherever at the head of some new undertaking you see the government in France, or a man of rank in England, in the United States you will be sure to find an association.[2]

In our work with American Philanthropic we seek to recover, to reignite, that tradition. For in recent decades, cultural, economic, and governmental trends have eroded civil society, as the work of political scientist Robert D. Putnam has demonstrated. Only by bolstering "social connectedness," concluded Putnam, can Americans restore "civic engagement and civic trust."[3]

Always, *always,* we are seeking to strengthen civil society.

■ ■ ■

Philanthropy—which finances civil society—has survived recession, depression, and war, but it could face an even graver threat today in the form of professionalization.

"Nonprofit studies," says Seton Hall professor Naomi Wish, is "one of the fastest growing fields in academia."[4] At last count, according to another Seton Hall professor, Roseanne M. Mirabella, 292 colleges and universities offer courses in nonprofit management, 168 schools of higher education have graduate degree programs with a concentration in the subject, and at the apex of this sheepskin pyramid sits Jeremy's alma mater, Indiana University, which in 2003 became the first university to offer a course of study leading to a PhD in Philanthropic Studies. (The first doctorate was granted in 2008.)[5]

Working backward from the PhD, in 2010 IU instituted a Bachelor's of Philanthropic Studies, and two years later the Indiana University Lilly Family School of Philanthropic Studies invested its Founding Dean. The department is peopled with men and women of goodwill, some of whom produce scholarly work of merit, and it graduates an earnest cadre of ambitious proto-professionals. Many go on to do laudable work in the nonprofit sector, but inevitably some alumni use the argot and secret handshakes of the philanthropic priesthood learned in school to keep the un-degreed in their place.

Concomitant with the growth of academic philanthropic programs has been the spread of organizations that certify those who jump through the proffered hoops. Typical is the Association of Fundraising Professionals, a New York City–based organization that, for a fee, will vouchsafe that the petitioner has earned the credential of:

- Certified Fund Raising Executive (CFRE), which is "a recognizable demonstration of your personal and professional achievement and commitment";
- Advanced Certified Fund Raising Executive, which "signifie[s] mastery of professional standards in leadership, management and ethics, at an advanced level of practice"; in other words, the ACFRE is for those who regard the mere CRFE holder as a rank amateur, barely more sophisticated than the legless blind man selling pencils on the streetcorner; or a
- Diploma in Fundraising, for those who "know the fundamentals—but you need to take that next step.... Don't just settle for fundraising as your job, make it your CAREER."[6]

It's too easy to mock the ridiculous humbuggery of this salesmanship, which reminds one of the back covers of old comic books ("Get rich selling seeds!"). Good and decent people enroll in these online and face-to-face courses because they want to get better at their jobs and climb the next rung of the office ladder.

But these are, at their root, pernicious. To the extent that these credentials privilege their holders in the pursuit of jobs, they act as barriers to entry.

The ultimate granter of the CFRE (Certified Fund Raising Executive) credential is CFRE International, which aspires to "se[t] standards in philanthropy" by handing out sheepskins to those who complete a written application and a written examination, and agree to abide by a code of ethics and standards, all for a fee of $875. On the off-chance that you flunk the test, a retake is just $375. To keep replenishing the coffers, the CFRE holder must recertify every three years.

CFRE International is based in Alexandria, Virginia, securely within the Beltway that strangulates Washington, DC, and the republic whose capital she is. But don't get the idea that this is some provincial American outfit. The CFRE disabuses Internet visitors with this answer to the question, "Why does your website use spellings like 'organisation' and 'programme'?" *Because the CFRE is a global credential, CFRE International uses British spelling, which is the international standard.*[7]

The flight from amateurism, from a philanthropy rooted in love and communal values, has been hastened by the federal government, in particular that bane of every American's April, the Internal Revenue Service. The instrument of harassment is the IRS's Form 990, which must be filed by all tax-exempt organizations exceeding a gross receipts minimum of $50,000. (In 2015, the most recent year for which statistics were available, about 295,000 charitable organizations filed Form 990s.)[8]

The Internal Revenue Service's revamped Form 990 goes far beyond merely ensuring tax compliance by nonprofits. They are required to report on their mission, leadership, activities, and finances over 16 separate schedules. The questions—Do you have a process for setting salaries? A written whistleblower policy? How is your conflict-of-interest policy monitored?—range from the nitpicking to the intrusive, but what they have in common is a complete lack of congressional mandate. Many are in no way germane to the IRS task of tax compliance and collection.

Besides the garden-variety harassment that is the raison d'etre of the IRS, these niggling and irksome rules seem designed to discourage amateurism in nonprofits. The Latinate root of *amateur*, recall, means love, a quality never in abundant quantity at the IRS. In recent years the word has come to denote one who undertakes an activity for no remuneration but the coin of love. An amateur need not be slapdash or oafish; Dorothy Hamill, Carl Lewis, Michael Phelps, and the 1980 U.S. Olympic hockey team were all amateurs. To despise amateurism, as short-sighted partisans of professionalism would have us do, is to contemn love and its often magnificent fruits.

The consequence of the IRS making its Form 990s ever denser and more confusing is to drive out amateurs. By requiring a specialized and sophisticated understanding of this gobbledygook—an advanced degree in application-filling-out—the tax agency is forcing more nonprofits to hire lawyers, tax accountants, and administrators. It is encouraging—nay, mandating—the bureaucratization of philanthropy. It is in effect waging furtive war on Tocquevillian associations.

The drive to professionalize fundraising and nonprofit management, to make it yet another field in which artificial barriers keep out the unwashed and benighted, from whom nothing is expected but deference, is consistent with the debilitating notion that an "expert" is anyone carrying a briefcase who isn't from here.

In fact, the professionals usually miss the heart of the matter. They tend to fall for whatever the latest fad happens to be. Today's conventional wisdom says that donors give out of *enlightened self-interest*. That is, they are driven by a desire for a good return on their investments. They are said to *prioritize*—and the use of that jargonish offense to the English language is usually a tipoff to the bureaucracy-blinkered vision of its user—*effectiveness* and *impact*. They look at the data, pore over the spreadsheets, furrow their brows analytically, and then they write out a check to whichever organization has the best *metrics* (another jargony word, and redolent of the system of measurement rejected with such gusto by Americans in the 1970s).

If donors aren't motivated to give for these reasons, the professionals tell them, they ought to be! This assertion lies at the heart—or, rather, the core, as there is no heart—of the "Effective Altruism" movement. (The term demands to be capitalized: no minuscules for these fellas!) But more on this conceptual forest without trees in a minute.

The late great historian Christopher Lasch, a social critic of coruscating brilliance, wrote of the ways in which "professionalism" tends to grow not in "response to clearly defined social needs" but rather as an act of self-justification. In field after field, the professionalizers "adopted a deliberately mystifying jargon, ridiculed popular notions of self-help as backward and unscientific, and in this way created or intensified (not without opposition) a demand for their own services."[9]

Ordinary men and women of sense and good intentions are incapable of mastering the complexities of modern institutions, goes the argument. Such mastery requires specialized education and expertise. In the interests of efficiency, the benighted many are advised to defer to the enlightened few. The result is a rational and effectual deployment of resources.

And if you believe that, we've got a Distinguished Chair in the Kim Kardashian School of Brain Surgery we'd like you to endow.

The actual result of creeping professionalization is the erection of barriers to entry, the discouragement of grassroots organizing, and the bureaucratization of charity.

■ ■ ■

To ensure the most efficacious possible allotment of resources, in recent years the professionals have devised ratings systems that reward those nonprofits whose practices track most closely with the dogmata of the professionals.

The rise of GuideStar and Charity Navigator—the leading umpires in the "empire of empiricism—the kingdom of counting, the sultanate of statistics," in William Schambra's alliteration—is understandable as a response to professionalization and giantism.[10] If you're directing your charitable dollars to huge impersonal institutions whose inner workings are inscrutable or even unknowable, then you might want to consult an almost equally huge and impersonal watchdog to ensure that you're not sending your money to sleazy swindlers or profligate incompetents.

The human factor having been excised from the meganonprofits—with the same results as occur in the amputation of a heart—these large and abstract organizations must be analyzed scientifically, statistically, with an overlay of business argot that glazes the eyes and dulls the mind. The industry becomes obsessed with numbers and impact and designs ever more abstruse ways to measure these.

The idea behind GuideStar, in the words of former CEO Bob Ottenhoff, is to enable donors "to make better and more confident decisions, which ultimately will lead to more money going to high-performing organizations."[11] Founded in 1994 in Williamsburg, Virginia, by Buzz Schmidt, GuideStar provides online information about 1.8 million IRS-registered nonprofits gleaned from their IRS Form 990s as well as other public documents. Most users access this information without cost; those wishing to delve even deeper using advanced searches pay fees typically in the range of $2,000 per year.

The IRS, remarks GuideStar vice president of operations Debra Snider, is "our biggest provider and purchaser."[12] This admission, or boast, belies GuideStar's pretensions to being a revolutionary force, for revolutionaries seldom boast of symbiotic relationships with national tax collectors. Jesus ate with the publicans, but he didn't trade intelligence with them.[13]

In November 2014, the Bill & Melinda Gates Foundation announced a three-year, $3 million gift to GuideStar to assist in the implementation of "its transformational strategic plan's three pillars of data innovation, data collection and data distribution." (Readers of mission statements are advised not to play drinking games triggered by variations on the word *transformative* lest they induce alcohol poisoning.) This grant was intended to help boost the number of nonprofits using GuideStar from 40,000 to 200,000, in accordance with the inevitably named document GuideStar 2020.[14] The practical result, of course, will be the elevation, in the eyes of "efficient" donors, of nonprofits that can afford a battery of attorneys and adroit form-filler-outers.

The hubristic geeks of Silicon Valley, having enriched our lives with Facebook and Twitter and other inventions of Gutenbergian magnitude, are determined to modernize charity. They're going to drag nonprofits into the twenty-first century, they crow, by designing better measurements of effectiveness.

David Bosworth, short-story writer, cultural critic, and author of the acclaimed *The Demise of Virtue in Virtual America*, has dubbed this obsession with measuring outcomes "quantiphilia."[15] Bosworth, a professor of English at the University of Washington and longtime resident of Seattle, has taken the measure of the Bill & Melinda Gates Foundation at close range and found it a nest of courtiers and flatterers, scholars-for-rent and "experts" whose expertise consists in reliably parroting the conventional wisdom on whatever subject is under study. The BMGF, to use its unwieldy acronym, scales new heights in the category of "billionaire donors with no local connections" who with cluelessly arrogant insouciance presume to instruct the locals in how better to organize their communities.

But humans are not machines, no matter how devoutly Bill Gates may wish it were so.

GuideStar's chief rival, Charity Navigator, uses an algorithmically derived four-star rating system, à la Siskel and Ebert (sans the wit of the latter), to grade nonprofits with annual revenues of over $1 million. Of course the late Roger Ebert graded movies subjectively, drawing upon a lifetime of erudition as well as visceral reaction. His intention was not to routinize and standardize the making of movies. Charity Navigator, by contrast, is premised on the belief that nonprofits need to operate more like businesses.

As the invaluable William Schambra put it in a debate with Charity Navigator CEO Ken Berger:

> Every organization grantmakers support now describes its programs in the rigorous logic of cause and effect, specifying that a "dosage" or "measure of exposure to its activities" will produce the desired effect—and submits statistical evidence that those dosages work; outlines a plan to collect such evidence in the future; and compiles a list of validating agencies that vouch for its work. And grantmakers require their grantees to "collect and publish feedback" from their primary constituents.
>
> Long gone are the dark ages when grants might have supported some young, passionate activist who wanted to start a movement from scratch; some professional disenchanted with the established procedures, yearning to try a different but purely experimental approach; some cause that probably was never going to succeed, but was worth supporting nonetheless because it was simply just and right. All such grants would have been based on mere feelings, on hunches, on subjective moral or religious preferences. None of them could have specified the precise dosages needed to inch the arrow along from clearly understood cause to clearly predicted effect.[16]

Quantiphilia, certification, credentialism, professionalism: If these are not quite plagues on the world of philanthropy, they are certainly drags. They complicate and confound; they dress what should be a straightforward endeavor in pompous empty verbiage and numerological cerecloths. They are relevant to this book only as negative examples, as lamentable features of the current landscape.

Don't let them distract you. Don't get lost in a forest of metrics. You have a better chance of successfully raising money if you follow the basics that we are laying out in this book.

Fundraising does require a store of basic knowledge, and like any craft your skills will improve with experience. But fundraising is not quantum physics. (We really should have a "Fundraising is not..." contest. It's also not orchid cultivation, Sanskrit translation, or a Nepalese vacation.) It doesn't require an advanced degree or an alphabet soup of letters behind one's name. Do the work, be honest, treat people fairly, be passionate, know your job, and you'll be just fine.

This is where the professionalization of the field has led so many astray. They begin to doubt their own instincts, to defer to self-proclaimed experts. They meet with credentialed fundraising consultants who charge them $100,000 for a six-month-long series of charrettes and other exercises in navel-gazing. At the end of all this wool-gathering they receive an action plan that is impossible to implement. Despite a considerable investment in time and money, they actually become *worse* fundraisers.

At American Philanthropic, we believe in one-day meetings. We emphasize the practical; our goal is to enable you to succeed at what you are trying to do. Thus this book is a citizens' guide to practical fundraising.

We are in many respects outliers in the field. We are not knee-jerk contrarians but we don't run with the herd, especially when it's headed for a cliff. We know what works, we know why it works, and we refuse to be hoodwinked by charlatans and managerial-guru mountebanks, even when they have chains of honorific letters after their names.

(My colleagues and I have logged enough years in graduate school to know that just as the race is not always to the swift, nor is the granting of degrees.)

■ ■ ■

American Philanthropic offers periodic seminars in fundraising, and we've been asked on multiple occasions why we don't seek certification for these training sessions so that seminar attendees can receive credit toward the dreaded CFRE.

This is a good question. Why not seek certification? What's the harm in doing so? Certification would allow attendees to work toward credentials as professional fundraisers and, perhaps, attract more attendees to our training sessions. There is a corollary to this question: Why don't we require our own two dozen or so consultants to obtain fundraising credentials? As mentioned earlier, there are over 160 degree-granting institutions with programs in nonprofit management. Many large public charities now require fundraising certificates or nonprofit management degrees as a condition of employment. The trend in nonprofit management is toward professionalization and credentialism. So why don't we get on board? Why not become, and beget, members in good standing of the professional fundraiser class?

These questions get to the heart of why we are different. We have often said, only half in jest, that we are the homeschoolers of fundraising. One of the things that we have always admired about homeschoolers is their indifference and even hostility toward credentialism. Over the years, the professionalization and organization of teachers created steep barriers to entry. Mastery of a given field or occupation became less important than certification and licensing. As the historian of education Diane Ravitch writes, in the early twentieth century "relatively small departments of pedagogy expanded into undergraduate and graduate schools of education. These institutions developed numerous specializations, such as school administration, educational psychology, educational sociology, and curriculum. Experts and professionals sought to create an education profession, which had its own preparation programs and its own technical language."[17] A century after the virus of credentialism entered the body politic, a majority of teachers today hold degrees in education rather than in the subject they are teaching.

Today, virtually no one teaches in public (or many private) schools without a teaching certificate. Are these teachers more qualified because of their certification than the teachers of several decades ago, who wandered the earth without teachers' certificates? No. One problem with licensing and credentialing, whether we are talking about teachers or fundraisers, is that it professionally qualifies people who are good at licensing and credentialing—good test takers and classroom jockeys—and not necessarily those who are good at the occupation being credentialed. Examinations rarely test the actual skills needed to be proficient in the field. Indeed, licensing and credentialing exams are often written by insiders who were themselves good test takers but not necessarily good practitioners. As a result, credentialism creates a safe harbor for those who cannot actually do the occupation for which they are credentialed. It gives them license to be mediocre. In the case of teachers, we have built an elegant and vast machinery for credentialing that is at once formidable and hollow.

Homeschoolers care less about credentials—either for teachers or their own children—than they do true education. We say at American Philanthropic that we value the Aristotelian notion of practical wisdom. For our purposes in fundraising, a record of achievement is more important than a document testifying to hours sitting in a classroom.

This point bears repeating: Credentials create barriers to entry. This is a problem for those who believe in a Tocquevillian notion of American civil society. *Anyone, anywhere* is qualified by virtue of being a citizen to raise funds in support of voluntary associations: churches, clubs, advocacy groups, co-ops, leagues, community centers, and so on. You don't need a credential to undertake acts of good citizenship!

There is an even darker side to this problem. The professionalization of fundraising coincides with a truly insidious move to discourage political and community involvement more broadly. For instance, in California, state laws now prohibit neighbors from collecting money to fight business interests in their communities or take on state government unless they file as Political Action Committees and, in some cases, register with the state as lobbyists. In other words, one must receive the permission of the state in order to fight against state policy. The aforementioned new IRS Form 990, which goes well beyond the statutory authority granted to the IRS by Congress, is invasive, paternalistic, and discourages voluntary associations.[18]

We further contend that the flourishing of graduate programs in philanthropy could create additional barriers and ultimately discourage participation in civil society by average citizens. Civil society should not be the province of only the well-regulated, certified, credentialed, or connected. And it should not be managed by the government. Civil society, properly understood, stands apart from both government and business as a prudent check on both. Our mission at American Philanthropic is to strengthen civil society. We can do that in part by taking down barriers to entry, not by creating or participating in them.

Do credentials create better fundraisers? If they did, that might be a compelling reason not only to seek affiliation with a credentialing organization but also to require it of ourselves. Many of us at American Philanthropic had considerable experience working with fundraising consultants prior to joining our current venture. Since launching our firm, we have become very familiar with other consultants in our field.

What is our verdict? Well, it is important to understand that our company was born out of a belief that most fundraising consulting is substandard and a good deal of it is fraudulent. With important exceptions (which is to say any of our consulting friends who happen to be reading this) our collective experience affirms this sentiment. Direct-mail vendors, for example, who charge their clients a retainer, creative, and per-unit fee, among other fees, are usually not acting in the best interest of their clients. But that fee structure is standard operating procedure and well within CFRE ethical guidelines. We don't do that.

We don't charge a per-unit fee on direct mail. Why? Because it would put us at odds with our clients' interests. The bulk of nonprofit fundraising "scandals" have to do with vendors exacting inordinate fees for their services. Certification has not stemmed these practices; it has instead created a façade of legitimacy that masks these unethical business strategies.

At American Philanthropic, we hire a lot of people who have zero fundraising experience. They lack MAs in fundraising, their achievement walls bear no certificates in Advanced Fundraising, and when they start with us they wouldn't know a house-file letter from a nail file.

It doesn't matter. They learn.

Professionalization entails the use of a specialized language: shibboleths and hieroglyphics that may be gibberish but that signal to others within the high priesthood that one is also an initiate, a member of the lodge. The buzzwords and mantras are like secret handshakes and passwords, but instead of gaining admission to the treehouse or the Masonic Temple one lands a job in the world of fundraising.

One of our former associates, Rachel Short, shares this experience with us:

A lot of nonprofit leaders ask us, "Will I receive CEUs [Continuing Education Units] or any credentials for attending American Philanthropic's development training seminar?" I get the pleasure of sharing with prospective clients (and even current clients): "No, you will not receive CEUs or any form of credentials for attending our graduate-level seminar." I explain to them our belief is that fundraising is not rocket science. It's doing the small things well and consistently well over time. How are you acquiring new donors? How are you cultivating those donors (e.g., moving your donors up the giving ladder)? It's amazing how many people I speak to while promoting our trainings and our services (at conferences, etc.) who say, "I have my CFRE. Do you?'"

Just the other day, I met a woman who works for the American Bible Society in Philadelphia. We started talking about the nonprofit sector, and one of the first things she said to me was: "I just received my material for CFRE, and I'm about to start studying. I'll definitely let you know how it goes!" I shared with her what we at American Philanthropic believe to be true: Credentials are not necessary to (1) become an effective fundraiser; or (2) build a successful fundraising program. I was not surprised when she responded like many of the people I've spoken to before—"Oh, that's so refreshing to hear! I've been beating my head against the wall with various nonprofit leaders telling me that I needed to get my CFRE yesterday." I'm not sure what she's decided to do re: the CFRE—I'm sure she's getting some pressure from her superiors to get "credentialed." But, more often than not, our clients/training participants share with us that our approach to fundraising is "practical wisdom" they wished they learned a long time ago.

Okay, so we don't give a toss for credentials. What does American Philanthropic look for when we hire new consultants? Let us first state emphatically, as it cannot be said often enough: We don't care about fundraising credentials or even prior fundraising experience. In fact, we often frown upon both things. We primarily value liberally educated, well-adjusted, practically minded people. We like consultants who can think on their feet; who recognize the need for systems and procedures, but who are not so blinded by best practices that they are unable to adapt, innovate, or change when new circumstances arise. As we say in our seminars, there is nothing mysterious about effective fundraising. It doesn't require special degrees or certifications. It's not an arcane priesthood with inscrutable rituals. Its methods are simple and easy to learn. It is more a matter of doing things consistently and consistently well over time than it is about any special body of knowledge.

Is there a body of knowledge that is helpful to know to become an effective fundraiser or to build a successful fundraising program? Yes. But it is far less than the volumes of fundraising books and degree-granting institutions would seem to indicate. American Philanthropic is practical. Ironically, the premium that we place on liberally educated fundraisers, practical knowledge, and hard-nosed effectiveness (doing what works) is at once more basic *and* more rigorous than the body of knowledge offered by the CFRE. Why would we submit to a lesser standard?

We hope this doesn't sound prideful. There are more than enough self-important blowhards out there in the fundraising world; it sure doesn't need any more. But American Philanthropic *is* different—the advice we give is not found in the typical airport-kiosk *Seven Easy Steps to Success* or *Management Secrets of Vlad the Impaler* book-products.

Now, contrarianism for its own sake is artificial and wearying. But when the conventional wisdom is so error-ridden, and its consequences actually pernicious, then it is the duty of every friend of truth to be the contrarian.

At American Philanthropic, we stand against such much-ballyhooed trends as Effective Altruism, outcome-based measurements, and philanthroglobalism. We see them not as refreshing new waves but turbid tsunamis that would drown civil society. They also grossly misread people and why they give their money away—which is the subject of our next chapter.

ENDNOTES

1. Henry David Thoreau, in *Familiar Letters of Henry David Thoreau*, ed. Franklin Benjamin Sanborn (Boston, MA: Houghton Mifflin, 1894), 165.

2. Alexis de Tocqueville, *Democracy in America* (Cambridge, MA: Severs and Francis, 1863), vol. 2, sec. 2, chap. 5, http://xroads.virginia.edu/~HYPER/detoc/ch2_05.htm.

3. Robert D. Putnam, "Bowling Alone: America's Declining Social Capital," *Journal of Democracy*, vol. 6, no. 1 (January 1995), http://xroads.virginia.edu/~hyper/detoc/assoc/bowling.html.

4. William A. Schambra, "The Professionalization of Charity?" *Philanthropy* (December, 1, 2003), https://www.hudson.org/research/3121-the-professionalization-of-charity-.

5. "Nonprofit Management Education," Seton Hall University Academic Server, accessed June 20, 2018, http://academic.shu.edu/npo/.

6. "Certification & Career Management," Association of Fundraising Professionals, accessed June 20, 2018, http://www.afpnet.org/Professional/CertificationList.cfm?navItemNumber=554.

7. "FAQs," *CFRE International*, accessed June 22, 2018, http://www.cfre.org/about/faqs/.

8. "Charitable & Exempt Organizations Statistics," IRS, last modified January 12, 2018, https://www.irs.gov/statistics/soi-tax-stats-charitable-and-exempt-organizations-statistics.

9. Christopher Lasch, *The Culture of Narcissism: American Life in an Age of Diminishing Expectations* (New York: W. W. Norton, 1979), 228.

10. William A. Schambra, "Charity Navigator 3.0: The Empirical Empire's Death Star?" *Nonprofit Quarterly*, April 5, 2013, https://nonprofitquarterly.org/2013/04/05/charity-navigator-3-0-the-empirical-empire-s-death-star/.

11. Phil Walzer, "Williamsburg's GuideStar Pushes Quiet Revolution," *The Virginian-Pilot*, October 31, 2010, https://pilotonline.com/business/article_45ffbe97-44eb-5481-94b1-6970fc564940.html.

12. Walzer, "Williamsburg's GuideStar Pushes Quiet Revolution."

13. Walzer, "Williamsburg's GuideStar Pushes Quiet Revolution."

14. Mark Hrywna, "$3 Million from Gates to GuideStar," *The NonProfit Times*, November 10, 2014, http://www.thenonprofittimes.com/news-articles/3-million-gates-guidestar/.

15. David Bosworth, *Conscientious Thinking: Making Sense in an Age of Idiot Savants* (Athens, GA: University of Georgia Press, 2017).

16. Schambra, "Charity Navigator 3.0."

17. Diane Ravitch, "A Brief History of Teacher Professionalism" (lecture, White House Conference on Preparing Tomorrow's Teachers, U.S. Department of Education), http://www2.ed.gov/admins/tchrqual/learn/preparingteachersconference/ravitch.html.

18. Also in California, the attorney general is seeking to require all tax-exempt organizations to disclose their donors to the state. Whatever its intent, this requirement's effect would be to make it possible to intimidate those who give money to unfashionable causes. Ironically, those subject to this sordid exercise in speech-squelching would also include the National Association for the Advancement of Colored People: ironic, because the California measure is flatly violative of the US Supreme Court's ruling in *NAACP v. Patterson* (1958), in which the justices unanimously agreed that the state of Alabama could not force the NAACP to disclose the names of its members and donors. "[C]ompelled disclosure of affiliation with groups engaged in advocacy may constitute [an] effective . . . restraint on freedom of association," declared Justice Harlan in his opinion.

Yet the anonymity promised today by Fidelity, Donors Trust, National Christian Foundation, and other advisory funds is not without its drawbacks, if not for benefactor then at least for beneficiary. We have a client, a faith organization, that receives a six-figure sum each year from an anonymous donor via one of those concealed-identity funds. This contribution, while greatly appreciated, constitutes over 15 percent of our client's annual budget. The mystery surrounding the identity of the donor is a real source of worry and consternation to the nonprofit's officers. What if the donor dies, or cuts them off? There is no way to cultivate this donor, to bring him or her into the life of the organization. There are no meetings to take, or friendly notes to jot, or hands to shake. Does that make less work for the president and development officer? Sure. But when you don't know where the money's coming from you don't know if or when the flow might just stop, precipitating a budgetary mess.

Chapter 2

DIRT: Who Gives and Why?

Why do people give money to nonprofits? This may not be one of the eternal mysteries that preoccupy mankind, but ask a roomful of fundraisers and you'll get a roomful of answers: to cadge a seat on the board of directors; to be recognized, to feel good about themselves; to outsource their ideological goals; to score a plaque; because their spouse told them to; because the CEO is kinda foxy; just *because.*

The philanthropic establishment, which we believe to be dense, obdurate, and wrong-headed, is obsessed with this question. Moreover, it vexes and perplexes them. They believe that people give for the *wrong reasons.* Their donations are not effective or strategic. They don't do enough research. They don't do their homework. They don't use the large corporate evaluators such as Charity Navigator and GuideStar. They are, when you get right down to the heart of the matter, *stupid!*

Their giving is inefficient; they're not getting the proper return on investment, or ROI, in philanthro-acronym-speak. They are not *effective altruists.*

Effective Altruism strikes the ears as an oxymoron, rather like *Practical Love* or *Scientific Affection.* Its advocates extol it as a social movement that incorporates "data and reason" into philanthropic decision making. Its prime concern is scale—the bigger the better.

An Effective Altruist asks, "Will progress on the cause drastically improve a large number of lives?"[1] If the answer is no, then the giving is ineffective, inutile, a waste of time and money. Global interventions are the desideratum; anything less grand, anything that sees individual human beings as something more than indistinguishable units in a sizeable mass, is puny, mingy, even contemptible. To "do battle against numbers," as Ralph Waldo Emerson said of New England reformers, "they ar[m] themselves with numbers."

Effective Altruists assert that "distant strangers" have as compelling a claim on our love and charity as do those nearest to us; if, via some involutedly abstract calculation, a computer determines that your $20 gift can be put to more effective use by an NGO (non-governmental organization) on the other side of the globe than it can by the cerebral-palsied woman next door, then the mathematically calibrated morality of the Effective Altruists demands that you send your check to the NGO and ignore the cries of your neighbor in need. (Perhaps in response to the well-funded campaign of the Effective Altruists, international giving by large American charities has increased while their donations to rural America have declined.[2] Silicon Valley moguls don't get feted at glitzy dinners for helping single moms in Oklahoma trailer parks.)

Indeed, the Gates Foundation practices what it cold-bloodedly preaches in this regard. Homeless people wander, uncomforted or unaided, outside the doors of its $500 million Seattle headquarters while inside the Effective Altruists plot and palaver about the most efficacious way to combat homelessness. The scene calls to mind the New Testament passage from Luke: "There was a rich man who dressed in purple garments and fine linen and dined sumptuously each day. And lying at his door was a poor man named Lazarus, covered with sores, who would gladly have eaten his fill of the scraps that fell from the rich man's table."[3]

If this sounds weirdly divorced from normal human feelings, well, the philosophical father of Effective Altruism is Peter Singer, most famous for his defense of infanticide practiced against handicapped newborns.

A recent report by the Packard Foundation indicted (in very polite language; this is the Packard Foundation, after all!) Silicon Valley entrepreneurs for failing to meet local charitable needs.[4] Though the individual giving of these new titans of industry had greatly increased over the past several years, 77 percent of vicinal nonprofits had revenues under $1 million, and 30 percent ran deficits above the state and national average.

"Why," asks the report, "aren't more Silicon Valley philanthropists directing their dollars toward local organizations and issues—as opposed to national or global causes?'" After all, "some of these nonprofits have offices just blocks away from the region's booming tech companies."

The problem is embedded in Silicon Valley's "giving code," which esteems "*effective* philanthropists" who are "'bigger, better, and faster' in their giving than the philanthropists who came before." Dismissing the provision of food, shelter, and relief to the poor and suffering as "Band-Aid solutions" that provide temporary relief, "they aspire to get to root causes and solve social problems rather than just ameliorate them." Who cares about feeding those hungry Martinez children down the street when you can win fawning press with a seven-figure donation to a mega-nonprofit whose mission is Eliminating Poverty? *Effective* and *strategic* become code words for ignoring mundane and tangible local problems in favor of abstract, large-scale issues.

We can illustrate what Effective Altruism is—and what it seeks to eradicate—with an example drawn from Jeremy's stomping grounds in Phoenix.

Pete is not his real name, but let's call him that; the homeless, no less than the rest of us, deserve their privacy. He can be found in Jeremy's neighborhood most every day. Often, he is sweeping the steps or driveways of local businesses. Rarely does he say a word unless you ask him a direct question. He is a veteran of the Iraq war.

A local diner feeds him, and some of the patrons chip in to cover the costs. There is a running "Pete tab" at the register, to which you can add whatever you like. Folks have tried to do more for Pete, including finding his family. But for whatever reason Pete hasn't wanted their help, and he steers clear of all official social service agencies.

Pete and the informal web of charity in which he lives are of small importance in the grand scheme of things. But they are important, in a way that is difficult to account for on a spreadsheet. No one wants Pete, or anyone else, to be homeless. But because of the compassion and love it has called forth, Pete's situation has, paradoxically, become a gift to the community. *Pete* is a gift to the community.

This scenario is helpful in revealing some of the Effective Altruism movement's limitations. In EA logic, not only does the charity directed toward Pete fail to solve his problems, but it is also (at least in principle) immorally wasteful. According to Effective Altruists, Pete's helpful neighbors are in thrall to *emotion* where *reason* ought to be their guide. And reason says that the time and money put toward caring for Pete should be directed to a cause where they can do greater good.

Doing good is what EA-inspired institutions like GiveWell and 80,000 Hours are all about. How can we do more of it? How can we direct our finite resources to achieve the most impact?

There is nothing new about these questions. In essence, they are the same sort of fundamentally technological problems that partisans of "scientific charity" and "strategic philanthropy" have been trying to solve since the mid-nineteenth century. In isolation, they seem quite reasonable.

But if we consider the older, fundamentally theological tradition of charity against which modern philanthropy has always contended, we start to see what is missing. The practices of charity first introduced in the Mediterranean's ancient Judaic and then early Christian communities were truly revolutionary—to the extent that new words had to be invented to account for the new institutions Jews and Christians created. These communities rejected the widespread and seemingly commonsense notion that caring for the poor, sick, orphaned, and widowed was wasteful and therefore stupid.

To Jews and Christians, doing good through works of mercy was how one became good, and thus worthy to stand in God's presence. For those inspired by this theological vision, there was obviously nothing wasteful at all about such works, no matter their impact. The result of this new vision was the utter transformation of ancient society. The formerly marginalized became visible, even uniquely blessed actors in a great spiritual drama.

The erosion of Judaic/Christian belief in the West has brought traditional charity into disrepute, at least in theory. But in practice things are different. As William Schambra has pointed out, despite the best efforts of many in the philanthropic establishment, only 3 percent of donors choose to give based on their knowledge of a nonprofit's impact.[5] And on a less formal, non-institutional level, communities keep unsystematically pooling their time and money to help people like Pete.

This kind of charity may not change the world in the most "logical" way, but it nevertheless has an important effect: It protects, preserves, and grows local economies of love. Effective Altruism leaves such economies wholly unaccounted for. And when followed to its logical conclusion, it is their enemy.

"Rather than just give the poor small sums on an ongoing basis, philanthropy aspires to do something more lasting and radical," such as "getting to the root causes of poverty and despair," explained Peter Frumkin in his influential book, *The Essence of Strategic Giving: A Practical Guide for Donors and Fundraisers.*[6]

Put this way, it sounds unassailable. Don't just give a hungry man a filleted carp; teach him how to fish. Who could possibly take issue with such a commonsensical idea? No less than Ben Franklin said that "if you teach a poor young man to shave himself, and keep his razor in order, you may contribute more to the happiness of his life than in giving him a thousand guineas."[7]

Alas, in attempting to eradicate "the root causes of poverty and despair," philanthropists have sometimes engaged in social engineering on a massive scale. They have lent financial, institutional, intellectual, and political support to such dubious causes as eugenics and the sterilization of the poor or those with criminal records.

Consider the philanthropists and philanthropic institutions (among them the Sage, Carnegie, and Rockefeller foundations) that funded the early-twentieth-century eugenics movement, which sought to eliminate "feeblemindedness," "defectives," and "vice" by coercively regulating the breeding of those they deemed unfit. In their view, which was so very *au courant* among advanced thinkers of that age, our attachment to *this particular person's dignity and freedom* must give way to the universalist goal of improving the human race. In the words of Harvard biologist Charles B. Davenport in a 1910 booklet, the "tens of millions" of dollars that "have been given to bolster up the weak and alleviate the suffering of the sick" ought to have been applied instead to "enable us to learn how the stream of weak and susceptible protoplasm may be checked."[8] (The human beings consisting of that protoplasm were not to be consulted.) "Vastly more effective than ten million dollars to 'charity' would be ten million to Eugenics,"[9] declared Davenport. The millions that eventually flowed into the coffers of eugenicists were put to such uses as promoting mandatory sterilization and discouraging immigration by the "inferior" people of southern and eastern Europe.[10]

Similarly, those who scoffed at soup kitchens believed that our attachment to loving and serving *this particular person in need* must be superseded by the universalist goal of ending poverty itself. As Robert H. Bremner encapsulated the Gilded Age debate in *American Philanthropy*: "When charity reformers criticized James Gordon Bennett's gift of $30,000 to a soup kitchen, the *Graphic* pointed out that Bennett's scheme gave 'all soup and no salary,' whereas professional philanthropy proposed 'all salary and no soup.'"[11]

The homeless man curled up in front of the Gates Foundation's gates testifies to the nonachievement of the goal of ending poverty via scientific administration—and to the endurance of this universalist fantasy.

The poisonous assumptions of Effective Altruism have permeated today's nonprofit world. Charity Navigator now awards extra stars to those nonprofits that measure impact. These Effective Altruism brownie points are increasingly linked to an organization's ability or willingness to engage in "results reporting." Ken Berger, the past president of Charity Navigator, says that nonprofits that follow such practices will "find it easier to attract funding than charities that don't. . . . This is what many donors are and will be looking for."[12]

No, Ken, they're not. The obsession with quantification, with numerating charity and calculating altruism as if they were baseball batting averages, is a vast exercise in point-missing.

This was driven home, like a stake through Dracula's heart, by *Money for Good,* a major 2010 study by Hope Consulting (since acquired by Camber Collective), which was subsidized by such dreadnoughts of Effective Altruism and strategic philanthropy as the Hewlett Foundation and the Rockefeller Foundation.[13] The purpose of the study was to discover why donors give and how they can be coerced, *uh, persuaded,* to be more rational in their giving, that is, to give more money to Hewlett-favored charities and less to "irrational" choices. For much to the chagrin of the study's funders, many donors fail to leverage their dollars for maximum impact, to use their lingo, and insist on wasting their alms on the local soup kitchen or the fundraising dinner for the lady down the street who is undergoing expensive dialysis treatments. The fools!

Our friend William Schambra summarized the stunning findings of *Money for Good*:

- ◆ "Only 35 percent of donors ever do any research, and almost three-quarters of these spend less than two hours at it."
- ◆ "Among those who do research, only 24 percent regard outcomes as the most important information."
- ◆ "Of those who do research, the overwhelming majority—63 percent—use it only to...confirm that the group they've already chosen isn't a total fraud."
- ◆ "Only 13 percent use the research to actually help them choose between multiple organizations, to make decisions about which is comparatively the better performer."
- ◆ "The upshot is that only 3 percent of donors give based on the relative performance of charities."[14]

Three percent. That's about the same fraction of people who believe they have had an encounter with extraterrestrial life. So, don't believe the hype! "Impact investing" is as rare as it soulless. And it is as uncommon as bumping into ET in the checkout line.

The vast majority—84 percent—of donors do little if any research into the "effectiveness" of an organization beyond, perhaps, due diligence to ensure that they're not giving money to charlatans and mountebanks. Most give because they have local ties, religious affinities, or a personal relationship with someone there. That's what drives people. We call them "identity givers." They're motivated by the tug of the heart, not the calculations of the head. They're heart givers, not head givers. (This is also true, to a far greater extent than we are led to believe, for the people who run charitable foundations.)[15]

In sum, the conventional wisdom is, as conventional wisdom often is, flatly wrong. People do not give based on a robotic calculation of which charity will stretch their dollar the farthest. "Impact" and "metrics" leave them cold; the bloodless patois of the professional fundraising class does not speak to them. They are not hyper-rational; they are human. And good for them.

The theorists and the mandarins of contemporary philanthropy, fortunes (which are never big enough) at their fingertips, shake their heads and view the average nonprofit donor with a mixture of condescension, perplexity, and barely disguised contempt. Why do these knuckleheads insist on giving money for "emotional" reasons? Or for misguided and outdated religious motivations? Don't they understand that atop the hierarchy of charitable giving sits the goal of Achieving Transformational Results? Given the chance to write a check for $100 to a national or international nonprofit that promises to achieve world peace, eradicate hate, or banish cancer from the planet, why would anyone in his or her right mind drop money into a country church's collection plate or buy a dozen carnets of stamps for a local hospice for the dying? You're only helping a handful of people—and those folks in the hospice will be dead soon anyway; what do they matter?—when you could be Achieving Transformational Results.

In their eyes, giving from a sense of obligation (like tithing) and giving for the needs of others are inferior to giving to satisfy your own emotional needs or out of hubristic desire to cure the world's ills. The truly enlightened donor gives to "save the country" instead of giving cash to a Salvation Army bell ringer. Love, it seems, is *not* the answer; or at least love of particular people, places, or things is not. Love of an abstract humanity or incorporeal social cause trumps mere love of flesh and blood (and fallible, and mistake-prone) people.

■ ■ ■

So why *do* people give? We're glad you asked.

There is no data-driven reason why a development officer or a nonprofit leader should buy the hype about impact giving. It's smoke-and-mirrors, a delusion passed off as fact by people who have a professional self-interest in perpetuating this specious bunk.

"Heart giving"—charity motivated by love and empathy and the Golden Rule—will continue. It will never be driven out by statistical formulas, no matter how loudly the Effective Altruists bray. Heart giving is consistent with everything we know about human nature from modern psychology and sociology, from history, and from the Christian and Judaic theological traditions.

What do we know about human beings that relates to charitable giving? For one thing, *belongingness* may be the most fundamental psychological need of all. No man is an island, nor, except in rare cases, does he or she wish to be rootless, unattached, a free-floating particle in a sea of humanity. We need to belong, to be a part of something larger than just ourselves. Contributing to an organization can nurture this sense of belonging—especially if the contributor has the feeling that she is doing something more substantial than merely scribbling out a check and mailing it to a remote 501(c)(3) with which she has no tangible connection. (Generosity with one's money and time also conduces to good health and happiness, as Christian Smith and Hilary Davidson of the University of Notre Dame document in their 2014 book, *The Paradox of Generosity.*)

Related to this, *identity* and *participation* are also fundamental human psychological needs that can be fed by charitable giving. In the act of giving, the giver defines, or refines, his identity, and achieves a closer connection with others. This is true whether the recipient of the gift is a neighborhood parochial school, a literacy campaign, a community symphony orchestra, or a think-tank dedicated to a particular philosophy of government.

Americans crave community. One of the brilliant thinkers of the twentieth century, the sociologist Robert Nisbet, titled his landmark book *The Quest for Community*, and one manifestation of this quest is charity.

People give in order to experience belongingness, to shape an identity, and to become more closely connected with others, and *not*, in the vast majority of cases, to solve social problems or change the world. To the dismay and disgust of the Effective Altruists, Americans prefer to donate to the local hospital or historical society, to public policy nonprofits or social and cultural organizations whose views they find congenial, or to men and women—neighbors, brothers and sisters—like Pete.

They give for localist reasons, for religious reasons, for philosophical reasons; they give to foster relationships and to build community. Never forget this. If you start talking metrics and results and outcomes to potential givers—at least those givers whose identities are not already wrapped up in such concepts—their eyes will glaze, their thoughts will wander, and you will fail as a fundraiser.

Credentialed fundraisers, like credentialed people everywhere, love acronyms: They create an air of mystery, of opacity, as if only a select group of initiates can understand the abstruse and recondite concepts they are peddling. They natter on about ROI so reverently one might think they're actually talking about royalty. But no, it's only Return on Investment, a term borrowed from business to measure profitability ratio. Very few donors care inordinately about ROI, even if they feign interest during a somniferous discussion thereof.

In fact, acronyms act to obscure what ought to be simple truths—or untruths. So in a spirit of subversive fun, we at

American Philanthropic coined our own acronym, the aptly earthy DIRT, or Donor Response Theory. (Yes, we conjured up a vowel out of thin air. There is no *I*, but we needed one to make *DIRT*.)

The fundamental premise of DIRT is that to be successful, we must approach donors as they are, and not as we wish them to be. DIRT is a framework to organize our thinking about fundraising. It asks several basic questions:

1. What kinds of requests or asks can we make of our donors?
2. Where does each type of ask put the focus?
3. What response does each type of ask tend to generate?
4. What type of relationship does each kind of ask tend to foster?
5. How strong are the resulting donor relationships?

Essentially, there are four requests a charitable organization might make of its donors:

1. *Save us!* SOS! We're going down! We can't pay the heating bill or the hefty consultant fees—please send money now!
2. *Lend a hand!* We're not on life support, but we could really use your help. Please? Pretty please?
3. *Invest in our work.* We are an efficient and cost-effective entity that is pursuing ends that you, too, favor. It is in your self-interest to send us money.
4. *Be part of our community or movement.* Work with us toward a common goal, whether that is supporting a school, a cultural organization, or a political cause. Stand with us. *Join us.*

DONOR RESPONSE THEORY (DIRT)

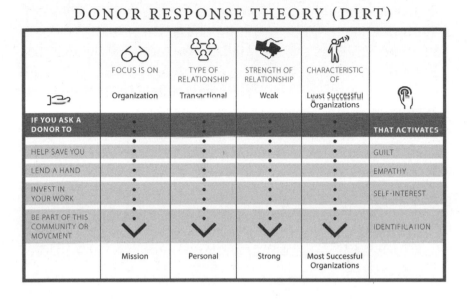

	FOCUS IS ON	TYPE OF RELATIONSHIP	STRENGTH OF RELATIONSHIP	CHARACTERISTIC OF	
	Organization	Transactional	Weak	Least Successful Organizations	
IF YOU ASK A DONOR TO					**THAT ACTIVATES**
HELP SAVE YOU					GUILT
LEND A HAND					EMPATHY
INVEST IN YOUR WORK					SELF-INTEREST
BE PART OF THIS COMMUNITY OR MOVEMENT	∨	∨	∨	∨	IDENTIFICATION
	Mission	Personal	Strong	Most Successful Organizations	

While the focus of the earlier requests (*Save us! Lend a hand!*) is on the organization itself, the focus of the latter two is on the mission. There is a cold, clinical feel to the third request (*Invest in our work*), which may have all the intellectual force of a trenchant argument but lacks any emotional appeal. The fourth request (*Be part of our community or movement*) is the most potent of all, since it invites participation in, and identification with, the organization.

A *Save us!* request appeals to feelings of guilt—I don't want to let these guys drown in red ink—and *Lend a hand!* to empathy, or shared feelings. *Invest in our work* appeals to the donor's self-interest. These three are *transactional* relationships. *Be part of our community or movement*, by contrast, encourages a sense of identification by the donor: It is a *relational* connection, which is deeper and more durable than the relationship formed by a mere transaction. The donor–donee nexus is much stronger, as the donor draws a sense of identification, belonging, and connection from the link. It's a tie that truly binds.

Our experience with hundreds of nonprofit clients has shown that these weaker, transactional relationships are characteristic of the least successful organizations; stronger, relational connections characterize the most successful organizations. Or to borrow from the Dutch priest and theologian Henri Nouwen, we misserve our donors if "we have not given them an opportunity to participate in the spirit of what we are about. We may have completed a successful transaction, but we have not entered into a successful relationship."

In practice, we have found that direct-mail appeals that ask prospective donors to join in a community dedicated to a common, external mission fare significantly better than do emergency, organization-centric, or self-interest appeals—at least over the long haul.

Moreover, as we shall explore in more detail in Chapter 6, donor clubs encourage increased giving because they provide an opportunity for greater participation and contribute to identity-building. Along the same lines, organizations that invest in relationship-building via meetings with donors and donor prospects grow faster and are seen as more effective by their peers.

So your goal as a fundraiser should be to make your organization a part of your supporters' identities: to become part of who they are, or conversely to bring them into the life of your organization.

The data back us up. When American Philanthropic surveyed over 100 nonprofits about their fundraising practices and outcomes, we found that:

◆ Highly effective organizations annually conducted twice as many donor meetings per development staffer than did other organizations.
◆ A higher percentage of donor meetings centered on an ask was *negatively correlated* with organizational

effectiveness. In other words, the fewer asks and the
more relationship-building meetings, the better.

◆ Organizations that more frequently communicated
with donors via house-file mailings experienced higher
donor retention rates. Donors like to hear from you—
and they should view you as a friend and comrade,
not a supplicant whose hat is always in hand and
whose favorite mantra is "gimme, gimme, gimme."

The fastest-growing, most highly admired nonprofits
invest proportionally more resources into cultivating real
relationships with their supporters. They understand that
donors are living, breathing people with hopes and dreams
and fears, not biped ATMs.

DIRT urges us to approach donors as collaborators in
a community jointly working toward some common good
rather than as mere investors in a social technology. It urges
us to think in terms of what Catholics call *communio*, the
essence of which is sharing, fellowship, and mutual participation. DIRT is very much in the Christian tradition. Whereas
secular philanthropy has, since its inception, been thought of
primarily as a tool for social change, Christian charity is different: It is an act of witnessing to God's superintending love
and our relationship as brothers and sisters. Social change
flows downstream from that. In the words of Pope Benedict
XVI, those "who carry out the Church's charitable activity
on the practical level...must not be inspired by ideologies
aimed at changing the world, but should rather be guided by
the faith which works through love."[16]

Whatever your own beliefs, donors respond best when
you act as if the premise of Christian charity—that we were
made by, in, and for love—were true.

The aforementioned American Philanthropic survey,
whose findings are besprinkled throughout this book, was
our attempt to fill a glaring knowledge gap. We had been
frustrated and not a little surprised by the utter lack of useful

measurements in the fundraising field. The numbers we found were not meaningful statistics—they were not like, for instance, baseball batting averages, which are a useful tool for evaluating performance. (Yes, we see the baseball-geek sabermetrician's hand waving in the back of the room. On-base percentage is more important. We get it.) Rather, the fundraising stats were as pointless as asking, "What is the average profit margin of an American business?" Framed this vaguely, and covering everything from IBM and General Dynamics to Pop's Ice Cream Parlor and Gary's Comix, the question isn't worth the breath it takes to ask it.

American Philanthropic to the rescue! Is that too redolent of Tom Mix serials or 1940s here-comes-the-cavalry Westerns and other cultural references that not one American in 100 gets anymore? No matter. Without bugles or fanfare, since 2015 American Philanthropic has surveyed, in great depth, hundreds of organizations to discover the answers to a quartet of questions:

1. What results are nonprofit groups getting in various areas of fundraising?
2. What variables are most highly correlated with organizational success?

And for our clients:

3. How do your fundraising numbers compare to those of similar-sized groups?
4. How do your fundraising numbers compare to other organizations operating in a similar sphere?

Few things induce yawns, lethargy, and inattention more effectively than an assembly line of numbers, so we won't overwhelm you here with our findings. We'll scatter them, when relevant, throughout the text. For now, let's just headline four of the major takeaways from our survey:

1. *Investing in development pays off.* For every hour of organizational time invested in fundraising, even small organizations raise $250, and the overall average is $500—over 10 times the cost of the average development hour.

2. *Relationship-building is crucial.* As just mentioned, the most highly effective organizations conduct more meetings per development staffer than their peers. Importantly, a far lower proportion of these meetings are asks, indicating that these groups invest in relationship-building, not just dunning for dollars. (We defined "highly effective" organizations as those which either were "highly admired" by multiple survey participants or had grown by more than 100 percent in revenue since 2009 or 66 percent since 2011, excluding organizations whose revenue at the time of the survey was under $500,000.)

3. *Direct mail is vitally important.* Groups of all sizes report that they receive an extremely high return on their investment in house-file solicitations, and the most highly effective organizations also invest heavily in direct-mail prospecting, even though their collective return-on-cost is average at best. The reason, in the latter case, is the same explanation that many spouses hear when questioning their significant other's expenditures: It pays for itself in the long run. (Though in the case of direct-mail prospecting, unlike party boats and new refrigerators, it really does!)

4. *There is underinvestment in planned giving.* Surprisingly few of our survey participants reported receiving more than a handful of planned gifts (bequests, estate gifts, trusts, etc.), despite the high average size of such gifts. This is a major deficiency that we'll address in Chapter 6.

There will be much more on these and other findings later.

The Gateses and Zuckerbergs and their flacks have done a masterly job of depicting themselves as magnificently magnanimous Medicis and Maecenases, and their foundations as veritable charitable oceans. The mass media, ever deferential to great wealth, have flattered them as such. "Let's ask the Gates Foundation for money!" someone is guaranteed to pipe up at the first meeting of any new nonprofit.

Yet this focus on plutocratic foundations obscures what makes American charity unique: the individual giver. These are a vital part—the head and heart and torso, really—of every nonprofit's fundraising portfolio. According to *Giving USA*, 71 percent of charitable giving in the United States comes from individuals; if we count bequests, that number rises to about 80 percent, with foundations contributing 14 percent and corporations just 5 percent of total American giving.[17] The genius of American philanthropy is not that rich people give through their tax-advantaged foundations. No; it's that people from every demographic group and income level give.

Although we'll discuss ways to approach foundations in Chapter 7, our focus in this book is on getting and keeping individual donors. Why? Because, as the epigrammatic bank robber Willie Sutton once replied when asked why he robbed those institutions, "That's where the money is."

ENDNOTES

1. "Introduction to Effective Altruism," *Effective Altruism*, accessed June 22, 2016, http://www.effectivealtruism.org/about-ea/.

2. Jeremy Beer, "Philanthropy and Rural Life: Diagnosing the Challenges," *Philanthropy Daily*, accessed January 24, 2018, https://www.philanthropydaily.com/philanthropy-and-rural-life-diagnosing-the-challenges/.

3. Luke 16:19–21.

4. *The Giving Code: Silicon Valley Nonprofits and Philanthropy* (Los Altos, CA: David and Lucile Packard Foundation, 2016), https://www.openimpact.io/giving-code.

5. William A. Schambra, "The Coming Showdown Between Philanthrolocalism and Effective Altruism," *Philanthropy Daily*, May 22, 2014, https://www.philanthropydaily.com/the-coming-showdown-between-philanthrolocalism-and-effective-altruism/.

6. Peter Frumkin, *The Essence of Strategic Giving: A Practical Guide for Donors and Fundraisers* (Chicago: University of Chicago Press, 2010), 2.

7. Robert A. Gross, "Giving in America: From Charity to Philanthropy," *Charity, Philanthropy, and Civility in American History*, eds. Lawrence J. Friedman and Mark D. McGarvie (New York: Cambridge University Press, 2002), 39.

8. Charles Davenport, *Eugenics: The Science of Human Improvement by Better Breeding* (New York: Henry Holt, 1910), 34.

9. Davenport, *Eugenics*, 35.

10. William A. Schambra, "Philanthropy's Original Sin," *The New Atlantis*, Summer 2013, https://www.thenewatlantis.com/publications/philanthropys-original-sin.

11. Robert H. Bremner, *American Philanthropy*, 2nd ed. (Chicago: University of Chicago Press, 1988/1960), 93.

12. Schambra, "The Coming Showdown Between Philanthrolocalism and Effective Altruism."

13. *Money for Good: The US Market for Impact Investments and Charitable Gifts from Individual Donors and Investors* (Fair Oaks, CA: Hope Consulting, 2010).

14. Schambra, "The Coming Showdown Between Philanthrolocalism and Effective Altruism."

15. Now, it is central to the identity of some people to think of themselves as "head givers." In cultivating such folks as donors, one must acknowledge and honor this fact.

Nevertheless, you will find that these donors are still moved by relationship, friendship, and communal belonging. They are not as robotically rational as they claim.

16. Pope Benedict XVI, *Deus Caritas Est*, December 25, 2005.

17. *Almanac of American Philanthropy*, 18.

Chapter 3

The Wending Planner—or, It's the Organization, Man

D o you know where you're going to? Yes, it's bad grammar, but Diana Ross, sans the Supremes, made a hit song of this question back in the 1970s.

For our purposes, though, it is the right question. Where do you, organizationally speaking, want to go? What do you want to achieve? You need a roadmap. It needn't be overly detailed; it can be scrawled on the back of a napkin—though we wouldn't advise that—or it can be more sophisticated, with goals and subgoals, weekly and monthly tasks, and targets to measure your performance.

Planning is basic to human endeavor. Do you want to boost your nonprofit's annual revenue from $1 million to $2 million? Unless you're out unicorn-hunting and stumble across the mythical benevolent billionaire dispensing million-dollar grants like a pool-boy handing out towels, you'll probably have to double your donor base. That means you'll likely need a direct-mail plan, a meetings schedule, and a calendar of foundation application deadlines. You'll need to draw up—and yes, this sounds like Business School 101 flimflammery, but it's not—a strategic development plan.

Fundraising consists of two primary tasks: Find new donors, and cultivate the ones you have. All else grows from these roots. Solve these problems and you'll never go hungry. But there are many ways of going, as a singer (not Diana Ross) once said. How do you find new donors? What is the most cost-effective method? What makes sense for *you* and *your* group?

We occasionally encounter clients who view fundraising as a necessary and temporary evil, something to be endured, to be gotten through, an ordeal and travail. Once they have run the gauntlet, they believe, they will emerge at the other end with enough members/subscribers/donors that the organization will then "pay for itself" and this icky business of raising funds can be dispensed with altogether. Incredibly, we've even seen this message in donor communications:

> Help us today and we promise never to bother you again!

This is, to be charitable, a phenomenally stupid idea. You will *always* be raising money. Accept this fact, even embrace it—or find some other field of endeavor.

Instead of searching futilely for end runs, do a few things—including direct mail—consistently and well over time. Mail regularly, with the understanding that acquiring donors through the mail pays on the back end, not the front. Repeat—Cultivate—Repeat—Express gratitude—Repeat—Meet with donors and potential donors—Repeat—Hire people with high social IQs. (That is, those with the ability to understand other people and their environment, read cues and nonverbal signals, and behave with wisdom and sensitivity in human relations. One person with these qualities is worth a dozen freshly tasseled CFREs.)

Set goals. How many new donors do you want this year and the next? How many small donors (which we might define as those giving less than $1,000)? How many major donors? How many planned givers? How many bequests? How many corporate donors? How many foundation grants? Planning is setting goals and then devising strategies to meet them. It is not wishful thinking and it is not powered by buzzwords. It is the harmonization of techniques (research; direct mail; grants; meetings; major donor clubs; planned giving; online giving; events; we'll walk you through each of them) with desired results.

We have identified five characteristics of high-performing fundraising operations:

1) Fundraising is integrated into programmatic activities and not treated as an afterthought or a separate activity.

In many nonprofit organizations, two cultures develop: a fundraising culture and a programmatic culture. This is crippling. At best in such cases, if infrequently, the two cultures exist side-by-side, going about their own business separately, hardly noticing each other. Their interactions are limited to grousing at the watercooler about the local football team's bum quarterback.

More often, however, the two cultures collide. Rivalry, mistrust, suspicious minds, and lack of respect degrade mission effectiveness. After all, as both the *Good Book* and a failed Illinois US Senate candidate reminded us, a house divided against itself cannot stand.

In a successful nonprofit, fundraising is not segregated or sequestered or quarantined; it is mutually supportive of every other aspect of the organization. Fundraising and programs are intertwined.

Rarely, if ever, does one find an organization with excellent programming but weak fundraising, no matter what the leaders of organizations may claim. You're only as strong as your weakest department.

Moreover, an organization's donors are often its best advocates. They are, to deploy a clunky martial locution, force multipliers: As donors increase in numbers and in giving, the organization becomes more effective at executing its mission. Or at least such is the case in well-run entities.

In poorly run organizations, the proverbial tail wags the dog. Development drives programming. Principles are malleable or barely existent; all that matters is the loot. More common, especially among smaller organizations, is for development to be treated as an afterthought. Other tasks seem more essential, or at least they do until the bank account approaches empty.

How can *your* organization integrate programmatic and development activities?

- ◆ Engage your leadership, both staff and board, in annual strategic planning. Here's where practical wisdom comes in: Invite the board chair as well as other board members whom the chair believes would be useful to have in the room; the disengaged, the doddering, the dullard, and those deep into their dotage can be discreetly left off the invitation list. As for staff, include everyone with significant decision-making power; Leonard the vaguely creepy IT guy can remain in his Ewok and Wookie-decorated cubicle.

◆ Call upon your program staff to participate as experts or organizational ambassadors in your fundraising activities with donors.

◆ Ensure that your development staff participates in programmatic operations and activities. Break down the walls; you're all on the same team, after all.

◆ Don't segregate knowledge or hide your light under a compartmentalized bushel; regularly report development and programmatic successes to everyone, creating a mutually supportive culture in which the broad range of the organization's activities are understood.

2) Practice the virtues of persistence, patience, and consistency.

Is there a more underrated virtue than persistence? Benjamin Franklin, one of the fathers of American philanthropy, said that energy and persistence conquer all things, and while the author of *Poor Richard's Almanac* deployed exaggeration as a stock in trade, good things come to the diligent.

Nothing in development is worth doing once. Successful development involves repeating a lot of seemingly little but necessary tasks over time. There are no magic bullets, no secret formulas, no winning lottery tickets lying on the sidewalk. Most requests for funding—whether through direct mail or proposals to foundations—will be rejected. "No" is just background music. But don't take it for an answer.

There are many reasons why a prospective donor or solicited foundation may say no at any given point in time. Successful fundraisers forge ahead anyway and create relationships, trying over time to figure out how a particular donor's interest or foundation's mission might coincide with theirs. They are persistent but tactful, indefatigable yet gracious, assiduous and shrewd. Many fundraisers give up too easily—on strategies, on programs, on people, on foundations, on relationships.

Trying for too long, past any reasonable hope of success, is rare. More often decision makers read too much into the inevitable failures that accompany any enterprise. They draw the wrong lessons—"Direct mail doesn't work for us"; "Foundations aren't worth the time or the effort"—cutting themselves off at the pass, as it were—or at the knees. Lacking a long-term perspective, they give up, thus sealing their fate.

Commitment is more than just a buzzword on team-building office posters. It's a prerequisite to fundraising success. Fundraising cannot be a footnote. It is as central to organizational health as food is to a person, fuel to an automobile, or applause to an entertainer.

You don't need to hire people with long resumes or years of fundraising experience. Hire smart people with good character and a strong work ethic. They can be trained. Raising money is a learned skill but it's not some esoteric art open only to a handful of initiates.

Doing things consistently and consistently *well* over time—sticking to it—allows you to assess with considerable accuracy what is and what is not working. It allows you to calibrate your efforts, not in fits and starts or in a purely reactive way, but in a thoughtful and measured manner based on experience. Hunches may occasionally pay off for desperate baseball managers who send .220 hitters up to pinch hit, but they're a recipe for failure in the world of development. So is a reliance on one-time get-rich-quick fundraising schemes, of which more anon.

Successful nonprofits do things consistently. They get their house-file letters out on time. They thank donors soon after the check arrives—soon enough in fact to please your Aunt Jane the etiquette maven. Their annual reports are issued annually.

Ralph Waldo Emerson famously said that a foolish consistency is the hobgoblin of little minds. Consistency is a goal but not a god; to persist in a pursuit that is not working and gives no hint or foretaste of future success is mulish and obstinate. We call it "legacy thinking," that is, clinging to outmoded or archaic ways of doing things simply because we've always done it this way. This can be just as dangerous as falling for its flipside, the insipid motto that "change is good." This absurd chestnut of pop psychology is obviously fatuous. Is *any* change, at *any* time, automatically good? Brake failure, a cancer diagnosis, getting fired on Christmas Eve, flunking out of school: Change is good? Unless one is a really perverse masochist or the most rigid contrarian, he or she will acknowledge that not all change is good. Neither is stasis, and neither is the foolish consistency in defiance of experience of which Emerson spoke.

But where consistency *is* next to godliness, and certainly no hobgoblin, is in those little things out of which big things come. For instance, punctuality: *Stay on schedule*. Don't miss mail dates; if a piece of direct mail is slated to be sent on the 15th of the month, send it on the 15th, not the 17th or 21st or sometime next month. It's so easy to slip and slide, to let a deadline pass unmet, to lose a day here or there and assure yourself that you'll make it up. You probably won't. And more importantly, you and your organization will become habituated to tardiness, to sloppiness.

Look: You don't have to run the place with military-style regimentation. Lord knows that the reigning style of the American Philanthropic office is casualness. No one punches a clock, lunches have been known to stretch past an hour if the conversation is good (or the service is slow), and the sound of laughter is even more welcome to our ears than the tat-tat-tat of fingers poking a keyboard. But we try like heck to hit deadlines, to get things out on time, to call when we say we're going to call.

Speaking of which, the failure to make regular phone calls to donors is one of those little things that derail a fundraising operation. And that leads to the next characteristic of a high-performing organization:

3) Involve supporters (and potential supporters) in the life of the organization.

As we explained while digging in the DIRT, few people decide to cut you a check after doing an elaborate cost-benefit analysis. Metrics, outcomes: These are the magic words of a cloistered and insular in-group, not the language of a man or woman deciding whether to support a particular nonprofit. Giving is not an irrational act, but nor is it a result of methodical ratiocination. Logic, we have discovered, makes for a sorry persuader. And this is true even among those who pride themselves on being stern and rigorous rationalists.[1]

For the vast majority of donors, having a substantial connection to an organization—a personal contact or relationship with one of its leaders, or an emotional identification with its mission—is *much* more important.

So tell your story. Let your donors and potential donors know what's going on behind the scenes, whether through newsletters, emails, phone calls, or visits. Give 'em a sense that they're getting the inside scoop. Hold events at which they can meet each other, for by bringing together kindred souls you nurture new friendships and a deeper sense of loyalty to your group. These events can be drives, campaigns, movements, and, as long as they're not too opulent, parties.

Remember that donors are trying to achieve your mission through their donations. They're helping you toward your goal, and in so doing they, too, are traveling the path. They are partners, not just funders. Treat them as such.

4) Build personal relationships.

An axiom among successful fundraisers is that "people give to people," not to machines, or abstract philosophies, or PO boxes, but to people. They want to give to people they know and trust. So any organization that is serious about strengthening its development program will invest in relationship building, especially with current donors. This is another principle that, once absorbed, tends to transform entire organizations, not just their development wings.

Successful nonprofits create opportunities for members of their target audience to forge connections. They do this by a variety of means:

◆ *Phone calls to long-time donors—no matter the giving level.* No, you needn't ring up the fellow who sent a $5 bill in a hand-addressed envelope, but fawning over the biggest contributors while ignoring those who give at more modest levels is not only evidence of a character flaw, it's short-sighted as well, for small but consistent contributors are the lifeblood of any healthy nonprofit.

The vast majority of gifts you receive likely will be under $500. A 2012 report by the nonprofit advisors at Third Space Studio found that donors of $1–$99 (43.2%) and $100–$499 (40.5%) made up almost

84 percent of the contributors to the organizations they surveyed. The munificent minority included those who gave \$500–\$999 (6.9%); \$1K–\$4.999K (6.5%); \$5K–\$9.999K (1.4%); \$10K–\$24.999K (0.9%); and \$25K+ (0.7%).[2]

- ◆ *Personal visits.* If your base is Santa Fe, you probably don't need to hop a series of planes to pay an expensive call upon a donor in Augusta, Maine, but to the extent practicable you should meet with the people whose generosity makes your work possible.

- ◆ *Handwritten notes of gratitude.* Have you forgotten those childhood lessons of cursive and courtesy? Relearn them. Handwriting is like riding a bike: It comes back to you, and besides, no one ever skinned a knee on a miswritten capital *G* or minuscule *z*. If the volume of correspondence is so great as to preclude handwritten notes, why not append, with a pen, a scrawled postscript? Believe us: It matters. And along the same lines, personalize invitations, using first names or even nicknames when appropriate. (This is all the more reason to get out and meet your donors: People are likelier to give to those with whom they are on a first-name basis.)

- ◆ *Non-solicitation letters.* Not every communication from you or the president of your group should be a request for money. Dunning for dollars has its limits. A brief letter summarizing recent happenings at your nonprofit and *not* asking for money is a refreshing change of pace. In fact, you should be sending such mailings at least as often as you are sending solicitations.

- ◆ *Emails from you, not an email blast.* Personalize email correspondence. The medium is impersonal enough as it is; sending the equivalent of a "Dear Occupant" letter is off-putting and counterproductive. The recipients are friends and donors, not marks and targets.

You don't want your emails ending up in the same spam folder as communications from "Canadian Pharmacy" and "Bored Housewife."

◆ *Listening.* Donors don't just pick your outfit at random and start sending checks. They've chosen to support you for a reason. You mean something to them. They're likely to have ideas about your cause or charity; listen to their suggestions with good grace and patience. You may well profit from their words, and at the very least you'll have solidified a relationship.

◆ *Use the language of friendship.* Employing words that bespeak more than a mere financial relationship ("friend," "partner," "member," etc.) presents your organization in a warm and friendly light. You're more than a stranger asking for money; the recipient is more than a target of supplication. You're both flesh-and-blood people who share a common interest. *Build a relationship.*

5) Do small things well.

Excellence is doing the right thing, in the right way, consistently over time. This is as true in fundraising as it is in swinging a nine-iron or cultivating gladiolas. Do the right thing, in the right way, over and over.

Often organizations let the little things we have just mentioned—a thank-you to a contributor, a follow-up call to a promising prospect, a house-file direct-mail letter—fall by the wayside. Or they focus too heavily on one aspect of the job at the expense of others.

The benefits of fundraising accrue over time. Small tasks, performed regularly, accumulate. The oak begins as an acorn. Those obsessed with bigness miss the individual trees for the forest.

Too often organizations put inordinate effort into trying to land the Big Gift: the mythical billionaire with an open checkbook who with one dash of his pen solves all of their financial problems from here to eternity. Good luck with that. But in doing so they ignore the little donor: the man or woman no one has really ever heard of, but whose modest gifts over time are substantial in sum—and who, by the way, may well leave a significant estate gift.

For instance, one of our clients, a magazine published by a nonprofit, received, quite out of the blue and into the green, a donation of $5,000 in response to a prospecting letter. The publisher had no idea who this woman was; she hailed from Ohio and had never, as far as anyone knew, so much as written a letter to the editor in the past.

The publisher responded—promptly. He called the woman and left, as is his practice, both his personal email address and direct phone line. She called back. They hit it off. Fast forward a couple of years: The woman, now a trustee of the nonprofit, gave $1.2 million last year—almost 10 times higher than the next highest donation. And all this came via direct-mail prospecting followed by skillful cultivation.

Don't mistake the small for the trivial; don't let the urgent crowd out the important. The truest path consists of many little steps.

■ ■ ■

We are members of Generation X. Perhaps for that reason, we are natively skeptical of most things, and especially of the planning that most nonprofits do: the navel-gazing, the team-building exercises, the fuzzy-headed plans put together by expensive consultants and filled with words like *ownership* and *stakeholders* that just grow moss on the shelf.

We like practical plans that have clear objectives but are flexible and adaptable in response to changed circumstances. These plans should be useful: a statement of glaring obviousness, but for the fact that many strategic plans are close to useless.

A *useful* plan gives your CEO or development director a roadmap guiding them toward their goals. It starts with an understanding of where you are now and where you want to go. We've had organizations with $1 million budgets whose leadership tell us that they want to increase that to, say, $5 million next year. We tell them that that goal is somewhere between unreasonable and preposterous, and unreasonable just left town.

More realistic might be a goal of a 20 percent revenue increase over the course of a year. That we can work with. The development plan will tell us how to get there.

To move $5,000 donors up to $10,000 will require face-to-face meetings. The rate of success might be 30 percent, so to move three of them up you'll need 10 meetings. One a month? Two a month? Three a month? Be realistic; don't set goals that you cannot meet. Don't pull numbers out of a hat (or an even less accessible place). Do the math.

Ideally, you'll have two planning documents. The first, for internal use, guides your activities. The second is an embellishment of the first: an external document, with an added rhetorical flourish, that can be used in fundraising. Donors are encouraged by the existence of such a plan, with its prospectus-like feel. It is solid, not speculative; saying that you currently have 100 donors at the $1,000 level and your plan is to boost this to a plausible 125 this year lends an air of credibility. It's doable.

As an example of a written strategic plan that is also a valuable fundraising tool, consider the John Jay Institute, a Philadelphia-based nonprofit whose stated mission is "preparing Christians for principled public leadership."

To the potential supporter, the attractively designed John Jay strategic plan explains:

- Who we are
- What we intend to do
- How you can help

A single-page executive summary states the Institute's "overarching vision" of "the restoration of American civilization" and then lists several concrete steps it will take toward the realization of that rather grand goal over the next three years. These include Philadelphia-based "intensive residential programs that form leaders intellectually and professionally"; a ramped-up public relations campaign; the enlargement of the Institute's donor base; and the hiring of additional staff.

A single-page "Brief Statement of the Problem" follows; the public realm in America, it asserts, "suffers from a dearth of leaders who possess the integrity, fortitude, and religious grounding essential to sustain a free and humane society." In response, the John Jay Institute proposes to "develop new leaders who are rooted in the wisdom of the Bible, classic texts of political thought, and the practical prudence and public virtue of America's greatest leaders."

Two pages of pithy explication of the Institute's mission and core principles follow, concluding that "an investment in the John Jay Institute and its students is an investment in the renewal of American society and culture."

The plan tells the reader where the Institute has been: There's a timeline, an organizational history, a catalogue of accomplishments of the young people who have received John Jay fellowships in the past. But the guts of the strategic plan provide an outline, with reader-friendly graphs and charts, of where the Institute is going over the next three years. It enumerates its envisioned expansion in the number of faculty, students, fellows, and recently commissioned military officers who will come to the City of Brotherly Love to partake of the Institute's offerings. The strategic plan tallies the proposed increases in events, gatherings, and social media presence. It offers a detailed timeline for development activities—the setting of goals, the devising of a calendar, the holding of development staff meetings, and the expansion of the Institute's donor base.

This is no wish-list or wouldn't-it-be-nice speculation; it has the ring of hard truth. It even recites the numbers for the next three years of the John Jay Institute's direct-mail campaign: The first year will see 25,000 prospective donors mailed, the second 50,000, and the third 75,000; the anticipated number of new donors acquired are 500, 900, and 1,300, respectively. Personal meetings with high-donor prospects are forecast to increase from 18 to 24 to 36 over the next three years, with comparable boosts in high-dollar solicitations and foundation proposals. The plan even describes cultivation methods, from personally signed thank-you notes to the establishment of a donor club. Finally, it proposes the hiring of three new staffers, among them a development director, to assist the Institute in realizing its goals.

The plan is meaty yet readable, and it deploys numbers without overwhelming the reader. It is illustrated with plenty of photos, mostly of people, not buildings. Staffers are pictured, of course, but more importantly, dozens of bright, eager faces adorn the pages; these are the John Jay Fellows who are being prepared for "principled public leadership." These young men and women are why the John Jay Institute exists; they are its raison d'etre, its heart and soul. Their miens mean as much to Institute donors and potential donors as any number possibly could. The implicit message of each photograph is: Your donations are helping *this person*, who in turn will help renew your country.

■ ■ ■

A robust development culture is as essential to a healthy nonprofit as rain is to a rose or spinach is to Popeye (or donuts are to Homer Simpson). In its absence, the organization will wither, sicken, stagnate, and die. When we asked our American Philanthropic colleagues for the telltale signs of *poor development culture*, our inboxes quickly runneth over. The most pertinent were:

- *A reluctance to incorporate development into organizational programs.* This is an especial temptation for those reliant on a sugar daddy who funds the bulk of their work. If said sugar daddy has located the fountain of eternal life, perhaps this trait won't prove fatal. Otherwise, the death watch is on.
- *Poor communication and a lack of collaboration—or even outright tension and hostility—between program and development staff.* One new client, whose mission was both timely and heart-tugging, ought to have been raking in donations. Instead, it was struggling to keep its head above water. We quickly discovered the problem: The program staff wouldn't even talk to the development staff, out of a misguided and absurdly snobbish belief that the discussion of money-raising tainted the whole enterprise. As a result, the development staff couldn't tell any of the stories from the field that made this outfit so compelling. (The staffs are speaking now, we hasten to add.)
- *Relatively few, infrequent, and unsystematic communications with donors.* We'll examine this at greater length a bit later, but we've seen nonprofits so indifferent or scornful of the basics of fundraising that they've received unsolicited contributions—people were actively seeking them out and sending them money—yet couldn't be bothered to follow up with or even thank these donors. (If ever an organization deserved to fail . . .)
- *A belief that the pool of potential donors is painfully finite or has already been exhausted.* Except in the case of extremely small or localized nonprofits, this is just *never* true.

◆ *Lack of investment in development infrastructure, including personnel, technology, and systems.* We know of one educational institution with ample resources— for now—that refuses to invest in staff or even elemental software platforms. Employees are overstressed, which may be good for vendors of Valium and Maalox but is terrible for morale. This institution still uses paper files as a donor database. If this were an example of living within straitened means or romantically clinging to the pre-digital age, we could respect it, but instead it's just cheapness, and cheapness, ironically, will cost them dearly.

◆ *Significant development staff turnover.* Not only is this a sure sign of a poisoned corporate culture, it erodes institutional knowledge and memory. Poorly informed staffers are notoriously ineffective at coaxing contributions in face-to-face meetings.

◆ *A belief that if the organization is on a mission— whether from God, à la the Blues Brothers, or for the betterment of humanity—and doing quality programming, the money will automatically follow.* It won't. Even Jake and Elwood had to reunite their band to save the Catholic orphanage.

◆ *The conviction that one or more of the major development tactics has been tried and shown definitively "not to work."* This is the excuse nonprofits use to avoid direct mail. As we will show, it's flatly untrue. Conversely, overreliance on a single fundraising strategy to the exclusion of all others is also shortsighted.

◆ *Leaders who have little experience or, more cripplingly, limited aptitude for business or nonprofit management.* There is a ready cure for inexperience: experience. Ineptness is more problematic. So is a reluctance to fully commit: the "I'm not really a president/CEO; I'm just an academic/teacher/humanist playing at being one" attitude. We dislike Bro-speak as much as the next literate person, but if you're not all in, stay out.

◆ *Reliance on a single individual (often the founder) to raise funds via personal contacts and charisma instead of building an institutional fundraising system.* Again, unless someone has unlocked the secret of eternal earthly life, this is a non-starter, or, more accurately, an ender.

◆ *Pervasive skepticism of the value and/or morality of asking people for money.* A down-and-out street-corner mendicant might wrestle with this question. A politician should, but won't. If your organization is doing good work, and your fundraising appeals are honest, you needn't have a single qualm in this regard.

◆ *Unwillingness on the part of an organization's leaders to delegate tasks and decision-making authority to staff members.* This is the dreaded micromanagement that is the bane of an employee's existence. Micromanagers are at least successful in one regard: They turn organizations into micro-organizations.

■ ■ ■

We've said it before, and before we've finished we'll say it again, more than once. There are two things every nonprofit has to do. Only two things, and if you do them well you'll be fine.

Task one: Find new donors. Task two: Cultivate and retain the donors you have. That's it. Do these well and everything's copacetic. Don't do them well and you're gone with the wind.

If you're not growing your donor base, something is wrong. Atrophy is setting in. You will, inevitably, lose a certain percentage of your donors through no fault of your own: *annually, approximately 40 percent.* They will drift away due to changing interests, or reduced financial circumstances, or the winnowing of the field by Time the conqueror. But a healthy nonprofit replenishes its stock. Nothing, and we mean *nothing*, conduces to this end better than direct mail.

We not infrequently have organizations come to us and say, "Look, we'd like to find 1,000 new donors, but we don't want to do direct mail."

Okay; how do you propose to do that?

"Well," they reply, hesitantly, "Ed has some friends who know some people...."

In the annals of nonstarterdom, this tops the list. We guarantee that reliance on Ed and his circle of friends will not work in the long run, and almost certainly not in the short run, either.

Don't shoot for the moon when there are plenty of potential supporters on good old terra firma.

Board members may play any of several salutary roles—guardian angel, conscience, devil's advocate, vigilant defender of the treasury—but they also have a tendency to give bad Ed-like advice, at least fitfully. A president of a fledgling foundation speaks of a phone call he received from a well-heeled member of the board of directors. In his world of high-stakes business transactions, the director said, $3 million deals happen much easier than piddly $20,000 commercial rentals, so why don't we forget about the nickel-and-dimers—that is, those who might contribute $100–$1,000—and set our sights on people who can write million-dollar checks?

The Benevolent Billionaire Philanthropist Who Will Solve All Our Problems (and invite us to cool parties) is the subject of as many fever dreams as Bigfoot—and seekers have notched about the same number of credible sightings of each. Godot is likelier to show up bearing a check for $3 million.

Don't concentrate your search on hooking one or two of those big donors who enjoy splashing around in the whale pond. This is a frequent reverie of cash-strapped nonprofit professionals: If only we could land Bill Gates/Sheldon Adelson/George Soros, then all our money troubles would disappear and we'd spend the rest of our days in high cotton!

This is a common nonprofit fantasy. It makes for a harmless daydream, but it's a sucker's bet. For one thing, it's about as realistic as the Cheryl Tiegs fantasies enjoyed by men of a certain age when they were teenagers. Cheryl was not going to walk through that door, no matter how ardently her presence was desired, and neither is Gates, Adelson, Soros, or another billionaire with a checkbook.

And really now: Do you want to plan your days around sucking up to a rich egomaniac who controls your purse strings? Of course not. You'll be subject to his every whim and caprice; your mood and the mood of your staff will depend upon his mood; he'll call the shots while you act as servitor, bowing and scraping and otherwise demeaning yourself, always painfully aware that if he wakes on the wrong side of the bed he can cut off your funding and put the quietus to your organization.

You don't want that. It stretches obsequiousness to the breaking point. It's positively un-American. Instead, broaden your base of support. Find new donors. Cultivate the ones you already have. Let a thousand flowers bloom in the garden of your supporters. You'll be much stronger: Not only will you not be under the thumb of an imperious plutocrat, but you'll have hundreds or thousands of advocates spreading the good word about your organization. Put those force multipliers to work.

We spend a good deal of time talking people out of bad ideas for getting major donors. Most of them are fishing expeditions in imagined ponds of rich philanthropists, or of the Ed-style "a friend told me about this guy" type. Now and then you may coax a check from the latter, but in chasing "this guy" down you ignore the far more promising pool of small-donors-who-can-become-major donors. Fundraisers would do well to remember: Just because someone is wealthy and is a friend of a board member doesn't mean that she is at all interested in giving you money. It's far more likely that the person already giving you a more modest gift would give you a bigger one if you asked and showed interest in her giving.

We often think of major donors as a stagnant category, as if by some inscrutable and esoteric process people somehow become major donors, and there's not much we can do to influence this development. That is not true. You can grow your pool of large givers. The tools are at hand, because by and large, major donors come from the ranks of small donors.

Pant and obsess over the rich and you'll not only miss out on the mid-range donors who are the meat-and-potatoes of your fundraising; you may also pass right by the caviar. For instance, Jack Templeton, the surgeon who separated Siamese twins, was a man of great wealth and accomplishment but he was entirely unassuming. He answered all his own mail and carried various documents in a brown-paper grocery bag. You weren't going to meet him schmoozing at the country club. Dr. Templeton donated $1,000 to an educational nonprofit in response to an ordinary piece of direct mail. His cumulative gifts to this organization eventually reached well into the seven figures. Yet if the development officers of the nonprofit had been off on a snipe hunt for rich guys, they'd never have raised that kind of money from Dr. Templeton; it was diligent cultivation and research that brought him into the life of the organization.

We're not saying that you should ignore board suggestions or brush off friends who offer tips, but such meetings tend not to pay off and extract a huge opportunity cost. The time you spend on a wild donor chase could be more profitably spent identifying those in your small donor cohort who are capable of significantly increasing their contributions. (We'll tell you how to do so in Chapter 7.)

Some organizations make it hard on themselves. They swing wildly for a grand slam, expending time and energy inefficiently, even foolishly. Instead of concentrating on the fundamentals, they waste their efforts on longshots bucking astronomical odds.

Forget that direct-mail piece or the visit with a donor, they say: Let's come up with the next Ice Bucket Challenge!

The Ice Bucket Challenge, for those with blessedly short memories when it comes to social media crazes, was a fundraising gimmick in which participants were filmed dumping cold water over their heads as a means of demonstrating solidarity with the late crew of the *Edmund Fitzgerald*. No, that's not right. It was to raise awareness of (and money for) the ALS (amyotrophic lateral sclerosis) Association, which earmarks monies for research toward a cure for what is commonly known as Lou Gehrig's Disease.

This was no top-down carefully planned campaign. Its origins are murky, though professional golfers seem to have been the first to dowse themselves with buckets of cold water as a way of raising money for pet causes.[3] The ALS Association cannily adapted the stunt for its own purposes and raised a staggering $115 million[4] while unleashing on the social media world over one million videos of charitable drenchings.

This was a lightning strike for the ALS Association: freakish and unduplicable. Despite their best imitative efforts, other organizations that sought to borrow or adapt the Ice Bucket Challenge ended up all wet and nothing else. You can't plan bolts from the blue. But it happened—just as it happens that some poor schlub will win the $1.5 billion Powerball jackpot despite odds of 292 million to one.[5] Hey, he won—why can't I? (Well, there are about 291,999,999 reasons why.)

That peculiar combination of laziness, innumeracy, and desperate romanticism which leads people to believe that their number is going to come up in tonight's Powerball drawing also encourages nonprofits to cast about for the next Ice Bucket Challenge, the next viral video, or the next $115 million windfall.

The Powerball approach to fundraising is virtually guaranteed to fail. It is putting far too many eggs in a very fragile basket. Or to use another barnyard metaphor, it is tying the success of the organization to the discovery of a needle in a haystack.

Shun the haystack. We prefer Friedrich Hayek, the Nobel Prize–winning Austrian economist whose work demonstrated the superiority, morally as well as in a utilitarian sense, of human action and spontaneous order over central planning. The former relies upon the dispersed knowledge of many actors, the latter on the limited knowledge of a single decision maker.

Searching for a needle, or Powerball ticket, or patron of Croesusian wealth is a Haystackian approach; far better is the Hayekian way of cultivating many donors and many sources.

What *Doesn't* Work

There are as many paths to failure as to success, and the former often allure the naïve. Don't be distracted by the latest-greatest new thing: the shiny toy, the gleaming gadget. That way lies megabucks consulting bills and flashy software that no one in the office has the faintest idea of how to use.

Utopia is not achievable; the perfect circumstantial confluence never arrives. Don't "spend your life waiting for the moment that just don't come," to quote the scruffy bard of Thunder Road. If you hold off on acting until the stars align, you'll be stuck in a holding pattern until the stars burn out and die.

So act—not rashly, not impetuously, not without forethought and planning, but act. You cannot win if you do not play.

Strong leaders lead strong organizations, but unchecked leaders can steer an organization down fruitless paths or even to points of no return. If a direct-mail package isn't working, for instance, the problem is not always strategy or execution; sometimes the product itself is misbegotten. We had one client, a respected think-tank, that went on what can only be called periodic benders. The president would become so intoxicated by her latest enthusiasm that she insisted upon placing it front and center in house-file mailings—even though every market signal known to humanity screamed that this issue was a dog.

The president, a supremely talented woman, was wise enough—usually—to draw back when she saw that the bucket coming up from the well was as empty as a Kardashian cranium.

One of the most intractable obstacles to fundraising success is *Founder's Syndrome*. The symptoms are glaringly obvious to those who work in afflicted institutions. The founder, or founders, of the organization understandably regard it as their personal property. It is the realization of their vision and their hard work. They may appreciate the more recent additions to the staff or board, but they nurse a (perhaps subconscious) resentment against these johnny-come-latelies. "Where were you when I needed you?" as the Grass Roots plaintively asked.

The founder may be a control freak. Not only does he want to see every letter before it goes out, he also insists on making niggling edits to ensure that every jot and tittle is, from his point of view, perfect. This takes time, and what with his other pressing duties, the control freak never quite gets to the letter. It sits on his desk. Weeks pass. He finally takes it up and makes like Maxwell Perkins, his red-penciled edits so extensive that the pages look like they've come down with a case of papery chicken pox. The inefficiency and delays are maddening and costly.

Or perhaps he is a tyrant: an amiable tyrant, maybe, but a tyrant nonetheless. This is his baby and he can't let go. He needs to call every tune. The board exists primarily to rubberstamp his ideas; if some contumacious soul begs to differ or stands athwart the founder's desires, the upshot is at best a glower, at worst a tantrum.

Most founders do not succumb to this syndrome, but enough do that it is a recognizable phenomenon. They clog and clot the internal passageways of the organization; they jealously guard prerogatives that are no longer theirs. They get in their own way, trip over their own feet, and drive staff, board members, and supporters crazy.

Why else do organizations or fundraising campaigns fail? Sometimes because they deserve to. Consider a nonprofit devoted to explorations of philosophical questions. Its major project is a quarterly journal of academic studies. Putting out a quarterly journal is not a challenge on the order of, say, publishing a daily newspaper. Grizzled editors with sweat stains under their arms and half-eaten stogies dangling from their mouths aren't usually barking "Get me rewrite!" or "Ten minutes to press time!" in the offices of quarterly journals of philosophical reflection. The pace is, if not languorous or even leisurely, at least measured. It's not an easy job lining up and then editing quality essays and taking care of the housekeeping duties attendant upon a journal editor, but it is eminently doable.

Well, the nonprofit quarterly journal to which we advert fell short in one significant way: It only published once a year! There was always an excuse—illness, tardy contributors, unreliable funding—but such consistent dereliction is inexcusable. The quarterly-turned-annual is headed for a state that philosophical ontologists might call non-being.

Patience is a virtue, though the quarterly's managers were putting a little too much trust in the patience of their readers. Flipping the coin, *impatience* is anything but a virtue in the nonprofit world. It leads to some of the mistakes mentioned herein: an obsession with finding a moneybags, a sugar daddy, a magic bullet, an ice bucket challenge that solves all your problems at once.

Of course you're chomping at the bit, wanting to grow your nonprofit and perform the good works envisioned in your mission statement. That's natural, and admirable. But don't expect results too quickly. Be realistic about what is achievable. Jeremy met a few years ago with the president of a small nonprofit. They conferred over the president's dining room table. The organization hadn't even rented office space, let alone a skyscraper cathedral or palatial edifice, which is fine: Few things are more off-putting to donors than the sense that a nonprofit executive is spending money on conspicuous acts of self-glorification rather than on the ostensible purpose of his organization. But in this case, the president said that he wanted to increase his budget tenfold in just two years: from $250,000 to $2.5 million. Barring a miracle, that just wasn't going to happen. Setting an unrealistic goal is setting yourself up for failure and demoralization. It makes you sound like a fly-by-night: like someone who's not in this for the long haul but only for whatever he or she can get in the short run.

If you're lucky, your grandmother used to tell you, "It's nice to be important, but it's more important to be nice." She was right. Kindness, courtesy, thoughtfulness, simple human decency: You can probably keep your ship afloat even if the captain lacks these qualities, but really, what's the point? In two thousand years no one, not even the shrewdest and supplest minds on Madison Avenue, has come up with a better motto for living than *Do unto others as you would have done unto you.*

And the funny thing is, heeding this advice turns out to be good for business, too. Few red flags are quite so ominous as high staff turnover. It suggests a poisonous culture, poor morale, and browbeaten subalterns simmering with resentment against imperious or tyrannical or indifferent bosses. Control freaks, micromanagers, and helicopter bosses hinder and hamstring till the result is mass hegira.

High turnover does not conduce to successful fundraising. Not only are you constantly training new hires, people who must in turn acquaint themselves with a brand-new professional network, but when those who are tasked with raising money for your group are dispirited or disgruntled, they are highly unlikely to take their jobs to heart. Work will be, for them, something to endure, a grim obligation, a confinement from which they are plotting and dreaming of release.

Even well-run nonprofits can sink morale with ill-advised office rules. One of our favorite examples of pointless and counterproductive pettiness involves a group for which we have a great deal of respect. Alas, in a wrongheadedly symbolic move, the hierarchs announced that henceforth, junior staffers were barred from using Keurig pods—which is to say that they were barred from drinking coffee in the office.

This was doubly stupid: Not only did it drive home to the younger staff members that they were second-class citizens, but the coffee machine traditionally occupies a critical place in the community of an office. It is a gathering place, a place of fellowship, of amiable chatter, of friendships forged, problems worked out, and laughter shared. The coffee machine bolsters morale; it builds community. To banish a segment of the staff from its environs is worse than petty: It is self-destructive.

Next up in our list of Don'ts: Avoid political fundraising consultants at all costs—because believe us, they *will* cost you.

Think-tanks are especially prone to this mistake. These consultants are primarily concerned with raising money for political candidates. To their chagrin, state and federal elections are held at two-year intervals, so to stay solvent between elections they sell their lists and access to their connections to nonprofits with a political or ideological bent, taking a percentage of what they raise.

It makes sense on paper, but in practice these efforts usually come a cropper. Those who give to politicians and those who give to think-tanks are distinct sets with limited overlap. The fundraiser has a relationship with the giver she is soliciting, but the organization does not. The fundraiser is an intermediary, but she is also an obstacle, a barrier to the personal connection that is absolutely essential to *your* success in building relationships.

A final word on planning. We see on a consistent basis a reluctance by nonprofits to use direct mail or hire development staffers. These are *not* decisions that highly effective groups make.

The data from the most recent American Philanthropic survey ought to be eye-opening to even the most heavy-lidded nonprofit exec. Consider "Mean Dollars Raised per Development Hour, by Organizational Size." The average raised per each hour spent on development was *$677*—or probably 15 times the average salary of a development officer. The smallest organizations in our survey (those with annual revenue of between $100,000 and $499,000) raised an average of $123 per development hour; the comparable figures as we ascend the scale are $231 ($500K–$999K), $327 ($1M–$2.99M), $655 ($3M–$9.99 M), and $1,572 ($10M+).

Organizations raise more money per development hour as they grow larger, but investment in development still pays for itself three or four times over among the smallest nonprofits. Hire good development staffers, no matter your size. Even the smallest organizations in our survey averaged $276,064 per development staff member. Again, the mean shoots up as the budget increases: $628,747 ($500K–$999K), $845,283 ($1M–$2.99M), $1,546,353 ($3M–$9.99M), and $4,606,093 ($10M+).

Of course, development staffers need prospects to develop. Their need calls to mind Sam Cooke's lament: "If I could meet 'em I could get 'em/But as yet I haven't met 'em/That's why I'm in the shape I'm in."

Well, we know how to meet 'em. Direct mail is the best way to secure individual donors. These are the men and women who will fund your enterprise and talk it up as vocal, passionate advocates. It is to this technique and these people that we now turn our attention.

ENDNOTES

1. For a superlative exposition of this point, read Jonathan Haidt's *The Righteous Mind: Why Good People are Divided by Politics and Religion* (2012), one of the most important books any nonprofit leader could read.
2. In a survey we conducted five years later, 87 percent of contributors gave less than $500. The percentages of donors giving at levels $500 and above were essentially the same as those reported by Third Space Studio.
3. Sumathi Reddy, "How the Ice Bucket Challenge Got Its Start," *Wall Street Journal*, August 14, 2014.

4. "ALS Ice Bucket Challenge Commitments," ALS Association, http://www.alsa.org/fight-als/ice-bucket-challenge-spending.html.

5. Niraj Chokshi, "How Powerball Manipulated the Odds to Create a $1.5 Billion Jackpot," *Washington Post*, accessed January 13, 2016, https://www.washingtonpost.com/news/post-nation/wp/2016/01/13/how-powerball-manipulated-the-odds-to-make-a-1-5-billion-jackpot-happen/?utm_term=.50383facb142.

Chapter 4

Direct-Mail Prospecting—or, Where the Donors Are

Eighty percent of nonprofit gifts come via the mailbox. And yes, we do mean *mail*box, for online fundraising, though it should not be ignored, has yet to fulfill the grandiose dreams of its promoters.

How do you find and cultivate donors? Direct mail.

Yeah, we know it sounds cheesy, maybe even vaguely disreputable. Direct mail vendors probably rank somewhere between street-corner Rolex salesmen and politicians in job prestige. Done poorly, direct mail can be offensive, absurd, embarrassing, ham-fisted, and stupid. Done well, it is the motor of your operation.

When we launched American Philanthropic, we didn't want to do direct mail. We shared the common (and not wholly irrational) prejudice against it. At first we hired third-party direct-mail vendors. We were astounded by the cost: They charged us creative fees, per-unit fees (they always want to mail more, more, more!), and markups on materials. Not only that, their work could be shabby and shady. So we decided to do it ourselves.

(A quick note on terms: You find new donors through *acquisition* or *prospect* mail, which we treat in this chapter; you keep and cultivate them via *house-file* mail, which is sent to current donors and which we'll describe in the next chapter.)

Direct-mail prospecting can be a hard sell to board members. They can be impatient. "Show us where this pays for itself in a year," they demand. Well, it may not. Direct mail is a long-term investment, not a one-shot deal. Rarely do you break even on the front end. Typically, a prospect mailing will return anywhere from 25 to 75 percent of its direct cost. It's in the second and third years and beyond that the donors you acquire through direct mail repay your initial investment—and more.

Acquiring donors through prospect mailing may seem at first glance a dubious proposition. Consider the numbers from one American Philanthropic survey:

The mean prospect mailing response rate seems minuscule: 1 percent even for highly effective organizations, and even that number represents a celebration-worthy achievement. Nor is there much variation according to size, as organizations with both modest and considerable revenue are grouped around 1 percent. That means only one in one hundred letter recipients responds with a check! Why not just buy a lottery ticket?

And here's another one for the counterintuitive file. The real eye-opener in the American Philanthropic survey was the differential in return on cost from prospect mailings: The figure for highly effective organizations (54%) is far lower than the 85 percent notched by other organizations. In our sample, the smallest organizations (those with revenue of $100–$499K) realized a 142 percent return on cost for prospect mailings while the largest ($10M+) were at 93 percent. (The smallest return on cost belonged to the $500K–$999K group, though the smaller size of the sample may have accounted for the anomaly.)

"So, wait a minute," says the reluctant nonprofit executive, quite sensibly. "You're saying that prospect mail has a poor return on investment, and that only about 1 percent of those who receive the mailing will even respond? What do you take us for, marks and rubes? Why on earth should we waste our money on direct mail?"

That is a good question. But there is a good answer.

The idea behind prospect mail is that you are paying to acquire new customers. This is an upfront cost that repays the initial investment many times over. In other words, the initial cost is less of a concern than the longer-range cost-effectiveness. Direct-mail prospecting is the most cost-effective way to systematically acquire new donors over time. For instance, those who make an initial donation of $1–$99 will give on average $115 over the next five years, and those whose first contribution is greater will give more substantial sums over that same period: $698 for the $100–$499 donors, $2,376 for the $500–$999 donors, and $26,449 for those whose maiden gift is at least $1,000. (In our American Philanthropic survey, the average prospect mailing gift was $166.61, with the largest organizations realizing the smallest—$91.97—average first gift.)

The numbers in the previous paragraph constitute the single most trenchant argument for direct mail. Prospecting letters aren't meant to be one-hit wonders: They are ideally the first "Would you like to go out with me?" in what will become a long-term relationship.

Once you get 'em, you've gotta keep 'em, as Sam Cooke said. That's cultivation. Predictably, highly effective organizations have a higher one-year donor retention rate (64.3%) than others (58.6%). Respondents to our survey reported an average 60.7 percent rate of retention, with the largest organizations ($3M–$9.99M: 50.9%; $10M+: 54.75%) faring the worst. This is probably due to costs inherent in the larger scale of their acquisition programs.

The same pattern held for two-year donor retention rates: The average was 54.9 percent, and the poorest rates belonged to the two largest cohorts ($3M–$9.99M: 44.9%; $10M+: 44.5%). Once again, however, highly effective organizations reported a higher two-year donor retention rate (57.9%) than did others (52.6%). So the highly effective groups spend more upfront on prospect mail, and see a lower return on cost, but their great success comes in retaining donors—that is, *relationship-building*.

Direct mail isn't...let's see; we've used rocket science, brain surgery, and quantum physics...how about Bill

Belichick's playbook?—but neither do you simply dash off a letter asking for money and send it to everyone you know. You'll have to contend with the following elements.

Schedule

How often and when do you mail? In our survey, nonprofits sent an average of five prospect mailings per year, with larger organizations mailing more frequently.

Direct-mail programs vary widely in size. You should probably start small, experimenting with how best to convey your message and in what form before you expand. If possible, send your first piece of mail early in the year. The sooner you attract contributors the more time you have to cultivate them for the end-of-year mailing, which is traditionally the most lucrative. So a January launch is preferable to a summer or fall launch. (Ripoff firms encourage you to blanket the universe with letters because they are paid by the unit: The more you send, the more they make. As a rule, stay away from per-unit vendors.)

Your Lists

To whom are you mailing?

Just as Hollywood hostesses covet A-list guests, so do nonprofits desire A-lists of potential contributors. You obtain lists by one of three methods: an exchange with another nonprofit; by participating in a co-op; or by renting, perhaps from a direct-mail broker—and some of the latter are shadier than a 200-year-old oak tree.

The best lists you can get are from exchanges with kindred nonprofits. The most desirable lists are those containing the names of people who have already given money through the mail to organizations similar to yours. Alas, these can also be the most difficult lists to get your hands on. Some organizations are possessive of their lists; their fear, apparently, is that charitable giving is a zero-sum game, and if Joe Smith (is it time to update generic names in light of onomastic and demographic changes? should we call him, say, Dakota Garcia?), who gives $100 annually to Charity A, is persuaded to give $50 to Charity B, then he will reduce his contribution to Charity A by like amount. This is not necessarily true, but you can certainly understand why productive lists are jealously guarded.

Direct-mail brokers typically will rent you mashups of the lists of several organizations cobbled together Frankenstein-style. These can be okay, especially if you need volume, but they are inferior to a good exchange list from another nonprofit.

A better option, usually, is to participate in a co-op program. The vendors that run these programs (Wiland is a good one) gather donor data from dozens, hundreds, or thousands of nonprofits and then use that data to build models that spit out the best donor prospects for co-op participants.

The worst lists consist of donors to political candidates. These are absolutely worthless and a waste of time. Never rent one—even if your nonprofit has a political orientation and the donor list of a candidate with congruent views is available. For many reasons, those who give to politicians do not as a rule give to charities in response to direct-mail solicitations. Political donors seek immediate gratification through elections with their giving. Charitable giving, however, has a longer time horizon. And those who seek immediate solutions through politics are perhaps less patient with the uncertainty of participatory democracy expressed through the messiness of civil society. Or perhaps the reason is that the coin of the realm of politics is coercion, and civil society, voluntarism. Whatever the reason, lists made up of political donors never perform well for nonprofits. Avoid them.

The Letter

No, this is not the great single by Alex Chilton and the Box Tops, but the missive by which you hope to convince the recipient to become a donor to your nonprofit. What do you say? How long do you take to say it?

The rules of the road regarding the latter are fairly settled. But while there is reasonable agreement on best, or at least most effective, practices with respect to copy, the former question has as many answers as there are direct-mail firms.

Unfortunately, direct-mail copy is often considered cheesy, mendacious, untrue, and embarrassing. The shysters and quick-buck artists (quick bucks for *them*, that is; not you, the client) have sullied its reputation. But there's a way of writing direct-mail copy that is honest, dignified, and not embarrassing—a way to do it that will permit you to look at yourself in the mirror.

A direct-mail letter is not an academic essay. You're not trying to dazzle anyone with word choice or style, high wit, or locution, though you certainly want it to be readable, maybe even compelling. If it's not well-written, you're not going to get much of a response.

As for length, the cynical answer to the question of length is, "How long can you drag it out?" The Talking Heads (the new-wave band, not the dispensers of conventional wisdom on Sunday morning TV talk shows) once sang, "Say something once; why say it again?"

David Byrne & Company were obviously not direct-mail mavens. The rule is: Say something once; say it a few more times. You may think you're being repetitive. Well, you *are* being repetitive. That's good—not in everyday conversation, in which case you'd be that guy who can't shut up and that everyone avoids, but direct mail, even in cases where we adopt a conversational tone, is not the same as chatting with your neighbor about the chance of rain or how the Red Sox–Yankees series is going (unless you're asking your neighbor for $1,000).

Avoid terseness, but also avoid excessive detail. Don't get bogged down in the mire. Readers don't care about the nitty-gritty of legislation, and they don't want a tour of your boiler room. Tell them who you are, what you do, how their contribution can make a difference, and then ask them for money.

Broader, mission-focused letters work best. Connect the reader to the achievement of your goal or the sharing of your principles. How is the work that you're doing making the world a better place? Don't ignore specifics—the sweeping language of the epic is going too far—but those specifics should illustrate a broader point, as should the vignettes you draw or the stories you tell.

Keep in mind that direct-mail letters are not exercises in logic-chopping. No one gives because they have been moved by a mechanistically ineluctable process from premise to conclusion. If there's one thing David Hume got right, we naturally put our reason at the service of our passions. The person tearing open your envelope is not Mr. Spock.

The letter should be a mixture of brevity and repetition. No paragraph should be longer than three sentences, and no matter what your English teacher may have told you in high school, there's nothing wrong with a single-sentence paragraph. In direct mail there's nothing wrong—and a lot right—with single-*word* paragraphs.

We ought to have ended that previous three-sentence paragraph with an exclamation point. Or *exclamation point!* Don't be shy about using frantic or excitable punctuation. Exclamation points are good. **Bold** or *italicized* words, sentences, and paragraphs can convey a sense of urgency or importance. Don't be shy about using them! (Unless the subject of your letter demands a certain gravity. A fundraising epistle for, say, flags to decorate the graves of fallen servicemen, or donations to ease the condition of the terminally ill, should be suitably somber, though short paragraphs remain ideal.)

The best length for an acquisition letter is 6 to 12 pages, with a sweet spot usually at 8 to 9 pages. This is a stone-cold fact. No one quite knows why. But the rule is inviolable. It always holds. Well, almost always. Occasionally a shorter letter will do better with a list of low-dollar donors, but longer copy in prospecting letters tends to give you a higher response rate and higher average gift. Longer letters work better with people who will give you a higher-dollar initial gift, which will snowball on average into multiyear gifts of significant size.

Eight or nine pages may seem inexcusably prolix to you and your staff, but remember: You and your staff are not the target audience. That would be sexagenarians, septuagenarians, even octogenarians—the 60s to 80s crowd, and we're talking *age*, not eras (Beatles to hair metal).

Many of these people are retired; they look forward to the daily mail. Believe it or not, they may read all eight or ten pages. The length lends an impression of substantiality, of permanence, of reliability. It assures the reader that you're not a fly-by-night operator out to fleece them.

Clients are often skeptical of our claim that the optimal length of a prospecting letter is eight pages. "That's too long!" they protest. "You'll bore the reader to tears." One such recently insisted that we test our hypothesis. That was fine with us. We sent out a five-page version, along with the eight-pager we recommended. What were the results? The eight-pager had a much greater return on cost (64%–30%) and a higher average gift size ($131–$80).

Length matters.

So does size—of the font, that is. Use Times New Roman 12.5 or, at most, 13-point font; older eyes will thank you.

House files can be a bit shorter, but you still typically don't want to fall below four to six pages, except in special cases.

Want bigger gifts? Use single-sided paper. Double-sided seems cheap and makes you look like you're running a bare-bones operation out of the nearest Staples. No one wants to give her hard-earned money to a here today/gone tomorrow outfit. Letters with single-sided printing attract substantially higher average gift sizes.

Remember that the purpose of this letter is to raise money. So don't be shy. Ask for money on page 1, or at the top of page 2 at the latest. Repeat your ask, using specific numbers, at the end of the letter as well as in the postscript. And yes, always add a P.S., and maybe even a P.P.S., where you restate your ask.

Make it easy for the recipient; let her know what she is being asked to do. It's all well and good to describe your organization, its mission, and its activities, but don't forget that the primary purpose of this letter is to raise money. So ask, and ask again. The interested recipient wants to know just what it is you're inviting her to do.

Include a reply form. Full-page reply forms bring in more money than tear-offs.

You want to build a relationship with your donors, even in this initial prospecting letter. The language should reflect that. Use phrases such as "You and I know that...." The more personal, the better. Not in a fake-chummy way, or a presumptuous and obnoxious manner, but out of a genuine desire to share your story with another human being whom it may profit.

There is room for experimentation here. If your president or the signer of your letter has a strong or distinctive voice, let it be heard. We have a client, an adoptive mother whose organization sometimes takes on child-related issues, who will use phrases such as "When I adopted my three children . . . ." This is good; it personalizes the letter and gives the reader a sense of just who the nonprofit's president is and why she should be entrusted with a donation.

Ken Myers of Mars Hill Audio has a distinctive voice; so does Jack Fowler of *National Review*, whose conversational, regular-guy style has proven very appealing. Peter Wood, who helms the National Association of Scholars, writes letters with such flair that supporters suggested compiling them into a book. These aren't generic voices from an aural cookie-cutter: They sound like real people, people you'd like to know, to hang out with. Cliché-besotted direct-mail ghostwriters can never capture this kind of authenticity. They always come off phony and calculated.

This is not to say that you need to write your own direct-mail letters. American Philanthropic, our company, has a stable of talented writers who compose first drafts of prospecting and house-file letters for the inspection of, and revision by, our clients. But they are sensitive to the different personalities, characters, and missions of the nonprofits we serve, and they eschew the bland boilerplate and "Gimme! Gimme! Gimme!" entreaties that give direct mail its less-than-stellar reputation. Try to arrange an interview between the direct-mail writer and your CEO in order for the penman to get a sense of the latter's cadence and vocabulary.

There is an Eleventh Commandment of direct mail: You can break all the rules as long as your letter is in a strong voice. Be true to yourself is always good advice.

Testing

Adjustments and fine-tuning are part of the game. Some pitches and some packages are bound to work better than others. You'll only discover this by trial and error.

What message is most effective? Should you write about the totality of your program and accomplishments or should you concentrate on one particularly salient issue? You might have an intuition or make an educated guess, but induction, not deduction, is the name of the game in direct mail. Send out letters taking different tacks and compare the results.

Test premiums in the same way. In fact, you can have a great deal of fun with giveaways of the "For a contribution of $100 or more you'll receive..." variety. These don't have to be elaborate or expensive. Sometimes we just ask our clients, "What do you have lying around the office that you want to get rid of?" ("Mel in Accounting" is not the answer we're looking for.) Ties and scarves bearing the organizational logo are always good. Coffee mugs are fine. So are signed copies of books.

This isn't a transactional deal; the premium is worth nowhere near the contribution. No one is going to up his donation from $100 to $250 for a mug. What you're doing with premiums is creating or enhancing a sense of identification. You're tattooing the organization on the donor: not with ink on his arm but with a scarf on her shoulders, a tie around his neck, a mug on his desk, even a paper or laminated membership card in his wallet. (You'd be amazed at how many people not only keep such seeming trifles but prize them. Again, it's all about forging the ties that bind.)

If you can get people identifying with your mission, you win.

The best mailings the Goldwater Institute, a free-market think-tank in Arizona, has ever done included a funky Barry Goldwater refrigerator magnet in which multihued (teal, yellow, red, and violet) images of a steely yet pensive Goldwater occupied all four quadrants. Recipients may not be able to identify fully with or wear on their sleeve the conservative/libertarian message of the Institute, but they can identify with the legendary Senator Goldwater and his

Southwestern-tinged vision of an America of rugged individualists. My wife's uncle wouldn't meet with a fundraiser if she were a cross between Raquel Welch and Mother Teresa, but the refrigerator door in his cabin in the mountains has a single attachment: a Goldwater Institute "Conservative Before Conservative was Cool" magnet featuring Barry G. in dark sunglasses.

The folks at the Goldwater Institute also understand that behind every policy debate there are real-live human beings with stories; telling those stories has been a key to the Institute's fundraising success. It's one thing to bewail in a prospecting letter what some see as the snail-like pace of regulatory reform at the Food and Drug Administration (FDA); it's quite another to set in the foreground of this critique an account of a young woman, full of promise and life, who is dying because she is denied access to experimental medicines that might save her life.

This very issue, which the Goldwater Institute dubbed Right to Try, illustrates an axiom of politically charged direct mail: In order for there to be an Us, we need a Them. Let's preface this by saying that decorum and conscience ought never to be discarded, and that there must be limits to the excoriation of "Them," assuming they are human beings and not cancer or Nazism or a devastating hurricane.

Right to Try was a Goldwater Institute–born proposal that gave terminally ill patients access to potentially lifesaving drugs that had passed preliminary FDA tests but had not received final agency approval. The problem, from a fundraising perspective, is that the proposal was *too* good, too noncontroversial. Only the most obsessively nitpicking regulator could possibly oppose it. Of course the terminally ill should be able to try promising experimental medicines if the only alternative is death. Who on earth but the most bloodless FDA drone could oppose it?

Right to Try breezed through upwards of 40 state legislatures with barely a dissenting vote. The "Us" was so obviously on the side of the angels that there was no "Them." And that put a crimp into fundraising.

With policy- or politically oriented groups, by saying what you *are* you are also saying what you are *not*. This is good. You are defining yourself. But without a Them, the definition is too diffuse, too nebulous, too all-encompassing. There's no yin without a yang, no night without a day, and, when it comes to public policy nonprofits, no direct-mail success without a designated bad guy.

Humor is underrated in direct mail. You might want to soft-peddle it if you are raising money toward a cure for a particularly gruesome illness, or for victims of violent crime, of course, but for the most part a smile, even a chuckle, mayhap a guffaw, encourages people to enter your world, share your vision.

Earnestness and excessive seriousness can be a turnoff; humor is a great social lubricant. When we tested a package for one client, the inclusion of a coaster with an image of Thomas Jefferson and an invitation to "raise a glass" to the success of its cause *doubled* the response rate.

So relax, smile, and have fun. A light heart and convivial spirit can actually be good for business.

Conversely, cheese usually misfires. So do cheap tricks. Including a coin or even small bill in a direct-mail package is deadly. The message it imparts is this: We are giving you a nickel. You are now in our debt. Please send us a check for $100.

This is at best desperate, at worst deluded. It's laying a guilt trip on the recipient, to borrow a phrase that reeks of the late 1960s. Scammers that exploit worthy causes (e.g., that of wounded veterans) like to play the requited gift card. Typically they'll send not a nickel or dime but a sheet of return address stickers. These are extraordinarily cheap to print but unquestionably useful. They are intended to induce a feeling of guilt in the one who opens the letter. Gosh, these paralyzed veterans are sending me address labels that I can use when I pay the gas or electric bill; I guess I ought to send them a little something in return.

This might work—once, for a small amount. The transactional nature of the exchange is so blatant that it actually discourages substantial contributions. The guilt-ridden sap who keeps the labels and feels that he must write a check is going to think, "Well, I guess I owe them a little something, but hey, these stickers can't have cost more than a few cents to manufacture. How about I write a check for $5?"

This is not how you want to build your nonprofit.

You can also test packaging. We prefer plain envelopes that don't scream to any halfway-savvy reader CAUTION: BUNKO ARTISTS AT WORK! Some of the dodgier direct-mailers like to disguise their letters in the official-looking red, white, and blue of the US Mail, or blazon IMPORTANT on the envelope. There are city postal districts that refuse to handle such deceptive mail, and the unsophisticated and credulous folks who are gulled by these tactics are not the pillars of a stable donor base, anyway.

This is not to say that teasers can't work. Some do. For instance, an envelope declaring (truthfully) SPECIAL MESSAGE FROM THE BISHOP captured the attention (or played upon the guilt) of its Catholic audience, who responded in large numbers.

And though we earlier cast aspersions upon fake-chumminess, there are, shall we say, prefab ways of personalizing an envelope. For a few hundred dollars you can turn anyone's signature into a distinctive font. This faux-handwriting on the outside of an envelope can persuade fence-sitters to at least give you a look.

One other tip: Avoid direct-mail vendors who prevent you from developing any kind of relationship with donors. Among our first clients was a one-woman operation that contracted with a direct-mail "caging" vendor. She had zero control over the letters and absolutely no clue about just who these thousands of people were who supported her organization. She simply received a check every month from the vendor. This may sound good—leave the driving to us!—but in practice it severed the president from her donors. She didn't know them, and they didn't know her. This was a recipe for a crash-and-burn.

There is no CarFax or Better Business Bureau to affix scarlet letters to dishonest direct-mail firms, but there are red flags. If a firm engages in any of these practices, run, don't walk, in the opposite direction:

- They promise that there will be little or no upfront cost for direct-mail prospecting.

Wow—what a deal! Most nonprofits have limited if not straitened budgets, so the promise of a free mailing is a temptation of Garden of Eden–like potency. The firm will produce and print the prospect letter and then send the nonprofit a check after deducting costs and fees. Why, it's a license to print money!

Oh, but there is a catch. It's hidden away in the fine print. It binds you to multiyear terms and contains a forest of shady provisions, such as:

- The direct-mail firm has total control over your donors.

You may not mail them, call them, or talk to them for up to two or three years after they have been acquired. The firm will mail the heck out of these donors till the carcasses are

bled dry. You are forbidden from cultivating them or moving them up the donor ladder. The lifetime value of such
donors to your organization is nil. And the dishonesty of this
arrangement reeks: Folks who think they're contributing to
your worthy cause are in fact padding the bottom line of a
sleazy direct-mail firm.

- ◆ The direct-mail firm has control over the copy.

If you hired someone to write letters or grants for your
nonprofit and he left for a new job, would he be able to sue
you if you continued to use language from those letters and
grants? Of course not. But many direct-mail firms sneak provisions into their agreements that give them sole ownership
of the written material they produce, which means that if you
ever drop this firm, don't even think about cannibalizing any
of the copy they produced for you. In addition, some firms
don't even let clients edit or inspect copy, so you have no
control over how your organization is being presented.

- ◆ The packages are always gaudy and complicated and
  the volume of mail is massive.

Some direct-mail firms pull off an unusual twofer: They
produce mailings that somehow look both cheap and complicated. The drawings and messages on their brightly colored envelopes are tasteless or dopey, and inside one often
finds tacky trinkets or perhaps a nickel taped to the letter.
These firms will urge you to send out enough mail to blanket China five times over. They'll even want you to mail your
lapsed-donor file from 18 years ago every other month. Why?
Because they're getting huge kickbacks from the printers they
work with.

- ◆ The text of the letter creates a false sense of urgency
  or uses deceptive tactics.

These firms are looking for the quick hit, the fast score. They don't mind using the discredited *SOS!* appeal because all they care about is the short term. To them, cultivating is for farmers; their goal is to squeeze the suckers and move on.

And that serves as the perfect segue to our next subject.

What *Not* to Do

One could almost compile a 4-by-7 paperback, à la the 1960s Charles Schulz Peanuts-inspired *Happiness Is* books, about bad direct mail.

Bad direct mail is a two-page letter saying "Help! We're dying! The boiler is broken! Our bank account has flatlined! We're subsisting on used tins of Spam we scavenge from dumpsters!"

We're not exaggerating; a struggling religious nonprofit recently sent out a house file to past supporters featuring an image of a scuttled and no longer seaworthy vessel. "Save Our Ship!" the letter pled, and while this piteous appeal brought in a few bucks, it will fail in the long run. None of those who tried to help forestall the sinking of the ship will become regular donors, nor will they leave bequests to this nonprofit *Titanic* in their wills. You can guilt people into saving you once with the threat of impending doom, but the vast majority of those donors will lapse. They'll avoid you the way a passerby might toss a dollar to a beggar, but then cross the street on his return, not wishing to be hit up again.

This is the lowest level of the DIRT scale, but unlike bedrock, it is incapable of supporting a superstructure. Panic is the flimsiest of foundations.

Finding and exposing bad direct mail is a bit like tracking down and broadcasting bad karaoke performances: It's amusing in a way, but also cringe-inducing. You feel sorry for the suckers who are gulled by these scams, but you're not quite sure how to feel about the perpetrators. Are they cynical thieves, roguish charlatans, mawkish mountebanks, or pitiful concoctors of hokey come-ons?

One of our associates recalls a series of prospecting letters from a Chicago orphanage. They featured a starving child, emaciated and pathetic, above a caption reading "Thursday night." The waif seemed on the verge of death: It was Dickens meets the Black Hole of Calcutta, but it was happening just a few miles down the road, at least for those who lived in the Chicago area. The photo really packed a gut punch. And the implication was alarming: If you don't send a check, posthaste, the orphanage might not have room for this poor guttersnipe, who would be left to fend for himself on the mean streets of the Windy City.

A month went by. Another prospecting letter turned up in our associate's mailbox and it featured the same photo of the same child with the same caption: "Thursday night." Either this starveling child had remarkable staying power, the orphanage was run by hard-hearted sadists, or the direct-mail company was resoundingly incompetent.

The orphanage letter was at best disingenuous, at worst a manipulative lie. And if that weren't bad enough, we've seen the same photo used by other organizations in their direct-mail packages.

Pro-gun groups are especially prone to absurd histrionics. Don't get us wrong: The authors are firm believers in the Bill of Rights, and that includes the Second Amendment. But what is one to make of an official-looking communication (which is stamped OFFICIAL BUSINESS just to drive home the point) that purports to be a NOTICE OF FIREARM RESTRICTION COMPLIANCE with a return address of "Administrator, Dept. of Communications," in Washington, DC?

Below this, in subscript, we read vaguely threatening notices in Post Office-ese:

POSTMASTER

If undeliverable as addressed please refer to Reg F010.4.1 or the official DMM

BE ADVISED

Response is requested within 72 hours.

Obstruction of the US mail is punishable by fines up to $2,000 or up to 5 years in prison or both.

Yikes! Who wants to run afoul of Reg F010.4.1? Even more ominous is the misleading impression created by the juxtaposition of the two sentences under BE ADVISED. The careless or unsophisticated reader might easily be tricked into thinking that if he or she does not respond within 72 hours, a hefty fine or trip to the hoosegow is in store. Get out the checkbook!

The text inside is hardly more subtle. Unless the recipient ponies up a donation, "Barack Hussein Obama"—you remember him—and his minions "will systematically disarm you, me and every other law-abiding citizen in the United States of America."

Overkill in direct mail is a judgment call. Certainly it's legit for pro–Second Amendment folks to warn of the confiscatory schemes of gun controllers, but it's beyond the pale to suggest that a gun ban is imminent when the writer (or signer) of the letter knows damn well that this just is not true.

There is a tendency, even among capable direct-mailers, to accentuate the negative, to paint a dire picture of the world out there, its skies portentous, its future frighteningly uncertain. Laying out the problem—a disease, a social ill such as

illiteracy, an objectionable ideology—in stark, even height-
ened terms, can be effective, but you also want to give
the recipient hope: a sense that the problem can be over-
come, the disease or social ill cured, the dragon slain. You
want, in the lingo of the marketers and consultants, to
empower them.

A California-based conservatively slanted research institute with which we work has had great direct-mail success
by framing its message positively, even though, from a
variety of perspectives, the sky may seem to be falling on the
Golden State. The institute's letters acknowledge California's
problems but offer solutions and, what is just as important,
a sense of camaraderie: You are not alone, the letters seem
to say; there are others in this vast state who agree with
you—stand with us, link arms, and let us proceed boldly into
a future that just may be better than we had, in our solitude,
imagined.

The Magic Button

As we've said more than once, we strongly encourage clients
to raise money by direct-mail prospecting. *It works.* Yes, it's
expensive, but it's cost effective.

Board members, especially those who rightly pride themselves on being vigilant watchdogs of the organizational
exchequer, or just plain skinflints, might balk at the upfront
cost of direct mail. They'll suggest what they imagine are
cheaper options using more up-to-date technology than
mailboxes and postal carrier sacks. Such as . . . you know it's
coming . . .

Online Fundraising!

Everybody's doing it, right? Well, yes. But how much does
it matter?

Nationally, some sources have suggested, online fundraising accounts for about 7 percent of total funds raised by

nonprofits. That's not much, but in our American Philanthropic surveys the figure is even lower: between 1 and 2 percent. Trendies and those who cannot let a day pass without solemnly invoking The Millennials play this siren song, emphasizing the comfort level of Millennials with the gadgetry of the digital revolution, but they forget that younger people are far less likely to donate than are app-challenged hoary heads.

Focusing your prospecting on email instead of the US mail is a major snare and delusion. The rationale is always the same: Just think of the money we'll save on postage and printing! Email is free; let's just e-bomb as many targets as we can. After all, don't people prefer receiving simple messages in their in-box to bulky packages in their mailbox?

No, they don't, not if you're asking them to part with their hard-earned money. The promise of online fundraising has not been realized, except perhaps for the ideologically galvanizing political campaigns of candidates like Bernie Sanders and Ron Paul. Certainly it has fizzled in the nonprofit sector.

And the reason is that *nobody opens those emails.* They go straight to the spam or junk folders. They don't pass the legitimacy test. The hype is just that: extravagant and oversold claims that have no basis in fact. If you want new donors, use direct mail: those eight-page letters about which everyone—and this includes us—at first thinks, "These are too long; surely you can say all this in three or four pages." But empirical studies demonstrate time and again that those eight-pagers on old-fashioned paper *work.*

Admittedly, politicians, or at least those whose job it is to fill the war chests of politicians, have occasionally struck online gold, beginning with Vermont Governor Howard Dean, whose longshot 2004 campaign for the Democratic presidential nomination caught fire over the Internet. Dean raised 40 percent of his $50 million campaign budget online.[1]

Four years later, libertarian Republican Ron Paul inspired a (peaceful) army of small online contributors to detonate a series of one-day "moneybombs" that raised several million dollars at a time via Internet donations.

The Dean and Paul examples suggested the vast potential of online fundraising, but outside the niche of appealingly ideological presidential candidates it has barely materialized. It can be an especially frustrating strategy for snaring new donors.

This is not to say that online fundraising cannot be a useful complement to more effective approaches. Our clients include several magazines of varying political hue, and they have had some limited success in raising money online from those who have *already* made a gift. The requisite is a strong online presence: a blog or website that gets a lot of traffic. If you have that, you should try a digital campaign several times a year. Be sure that your most popular bloggers mention the campaign and post appeals for donations. Banner the site with proclamations of the campaign, complete with start/end dates and goals.

The most successful online campaigns we have run have been conducted in bursts consisting of a series of communications in which the goals are clearly articulated. Each successive email and social-media post provides an update on the progress of the campaign and offers a new piece of information—perhaps an announcement of an upcoming conference or program. These campaigns often don't pull in a lot of new donors, but they can be surprisingly effective in raising money from existing supporters. As a footnote, don't rent email lists (unless you're a political candidate). We've tried it, and without exception they have proved monumental disappointments.

What about Facebook and the obsessively touted social-media network? Things are changing fast, and perhaps in the near future Facebook may prove useful in acquiring new donors, but right now, it's a secondary or tertiary tactic at best. According to a study by the fundraising-software firm Blackbaud, social media account for a meager 1 percent of online fundraising.[2] As John Haydon, author of *Facebook Marketing for Dummies*, told the *Chronicle of Philanthropy*, "Very rarely would you pull out your credit card when you're on Facebook. People are going there to connect with friends or relieve boredom or avoid work. It's not about making donations."[3]

Dialing technology back a few decades, we've had clients who wanted to do telephone solicitations. Colleges do it, often with students calling alumni. That adds a sentimental twist to the ask: A bright, eager, bushy-tailed freshman is calling the graying grad, who may assume an almost avuncular role in the conversation. "How are things at good old Tech?" he asks, and the freshman tells him all about the new science building, the ancient oak trees on the Quad, the promising new quarterback on the football team.

Telephone prospecting for nonprofits is different. For one thing, a stranger is calling, not a nice young person from one's alma mater. There is no personal connection; this is just another solicitation. Worse, although the rates they charge are inexpensive, the phone-call vendors typically own the names. As with direct mail, it is unwise to deal with your contributors through a third-party vendor.

Okay, so you've prospected, and while you didn't hit the Comstock Lode, your direct-mail package brought in dozens, or hundreds, or thousands, of new donors. Now what?

ENDNOTES

1. Bill Scher, "4 Ways Howard Dean Changed American Politics," *The Week*, June 21, 2013, http://theweek.com/articles/462922/4-ways-howard-dean-changed-american-politics.

2. Thomas Held, "Charities Like Facebook for Rallying Support but Not Much for Fundraising," *Chronicle of Philanthropy* (July 13, 2014).

3. Ibid.

Chapter 5

Cultivating Your Donor Garden: From Thank-Yous to House Files

There is a somewhat macabre pyramid that depicts the evolution of a donor to your organization. At its base is the vast sea of prospects out of which you, to swim briefly in the aquatic metaphor, hook him. But pyramids are not liquid, so the subsequent blocks on the way up the pyramid are solid: letters of gratitude, cultivation through the mail, personal meetings, donor clubs, events, planned giving, and, at the peak, death and the consequent bequest.

It looks inexorable. It's not. Even the most successful non-profits will lose over one-half of first-time givers. Lose too many and you'll close shop.

So how do you turn a one-time donor into a persistent patron? Let us count the ways....

The first thing you do is the same thing your mother taught you when you were a child receiving a birthday present: *You say thanks.*

You have to have a gratitude policy. The term strikes the ears harshly, doesn't it? It's like a *love protocol* or *kindness rules*. But it is necessary. It should be clear and followed to a *T*.

Few things are more irritating than not being thanked for a gift, yet you'd be surprised how many nonprofits are derelict in this basic duty. Whether it's a sign of mismanagement or ingratitude or poor childhood training, the failure to extend this commonest of courtesies is self-defeating: The unthanked are unlikely to come back for another round.

Donor Acknowledgment

What ten-year-old hasn't grumbled through the ordeal of writing thank-you letters to the aunts and uncles and grandparents who shower him with checks and savings bonds each birthday? Etiquette standards have eroded over recent decades, and the thank-you letter has gone the way of the malted shop and the pay phone, but it remains a practice both polite and wise to formally express gratitude to those who have gifted you with presents.

This is no less true in the nonprofit world. Thanking donors for their gifts in a personal and timely way is an essential but oft-overlooked element in building solid relationships—and, not coincidentally, it conduces to healthy retention rates.

Acknowledging gifts should not be approached merely as a courtesy, a routinized duty, or, even worse, a transactional dispensing of tax-exemption information. Antiseptic form letters whose only purpose is to act as proof of a deductible donation are bad manners and poor practice. The thank-you process is a key step in strengthening relationships with the folks whose donations are your lifeblood. If done well, it can bring them deeper into the life of your organization, as they renew and upgrade their commitment. Over the long term, the genuineness of your thank-yous will pay dividends both fiscal and psychic.

Step back for a moment. Consider, with an appropriate sense of wonder, what a charitable contribution signifies. Someone—not your mother, or a person who owes you a favor, but usually a man or woman with only a brief or tenuous connection to your organization—has *freely* given you a portion of his or her hard-earned money, in return for nothing concrete or specific. That's remarkable, isn't it? What an occasion for thankfulness. It's also, in many ways, unique to the American experience. It's an act fitting squarely into one of the proudest traditions of our history. We should convey our sense of wonder and amazement in thanking donors, regardless of the amount given. Perhaps the giver of $25 won't receive a meeting request, but it's a simple thing to personalize her thank-you note. And not to put too fine a point on it, but that $25 donor, if made to feel welcome, may well become a $100 or $1,000 donor next year. God loves a cheerful giver; a cheerful giver loves a grateful recipient.

As in so much of life, timing is all. Promptitude matters. The 18-year-old who finally scratches out a rote thank-you for his graduation presents in October does not impress us. Nor does the slacker who cashes the check but can't be bothered to drop us a line. Likewise, the donor to your nonprofit whose gift is not acknowledged within a week or two (at the utmost) of its receipt is likely to be annoyed by what he considers your cavalier treatment of him. If too much time goes by, he may only vaguely recall making the gift. In any event, he will be none too eager for a reprise.

Thank Your Donors—and Thank Them as Soon as Possible

You should have a plan in place for recognizing gifts. Don't figure this out on the fly, or respond on an ad hoc basis. Know beforehand who is going to recognize the gift, when it will be recognized, and how it will be recognized.

A thank-you procedure—no, let's scrap that term, which numbs gratitude in the deadening language of bureaucracy— just plain thank-yous should be executable, personal, tiered according to the level of donation, and performed in a consistent manner. Don't just feed them through a generic thank-you blender. First-time donors should be thanked differently from those house-file donors who have given to your organization before. The general rule is that those who give more money (whether in a single gift, over time, or even if that greater gift is a potentiality rather than current reality) should receive more personalized attention. But that doesn't mean that you should neglect or slight low-dollar donors. The Gospel story of the widow's mite is instructive, but even on a cold-bloodedly utilitarian level it's worth your while to treat the $15 donor with respect.

Steven Shattuck, vice president of marketing at the Indiana-based nonprofit consultancy Bloomerang, explains in a perceptive article ("Why Small Donations Should Matter a Lot to Nonprofits") how to cultivate those who give at what some might scornfully consider a pittance level.[1] Those of limited means, says Shattuck, might make valuable volunteers or ambassadors; other pocket-change donors might just be feeling you out, dipping a toe in the water before taking a plunge—and if their modest gift is either ignored or acknowledged via a cold email receipt they may well leave for more congenial pools.

As Shattuck says, you don't need to throw a gala or order an engraved brick paver for the $15 donor. But a quick handwritten note, personalized letter, or acknowledgement via Twitter or LinkedIn just might sow the seeds of a fecund relationship in the future.

The nonprofit world abounds with stories of donors who gave modest annual gifts of $50 or even less and then left six- or seven-figure planned gifts upon their death. That doesn't mean that every low-level donor is a fat bequest in waiting—nor should one cynically treat them as such—but as the New York State Lotto ads say, "Hey . . . ya never know."

For smaller gifts, a thank-you letter should be sent within a week of the gift's receipt. (Higher-dollar donors who get phone calls should also receive letters.) Donors contributing above a certain level should receive a handwritten personal note from the executive director or major gifts officer, who should have a stack of thank-you letters or cards on her desk. You can include their legal tax receipt in the thank-you letter, though some organizations prefer to mail these at year's end.

As a rule, discrete $100 and $1,000 gifts should trigger additional attention. So should gifts through donor-advised funds, foundations, or special checking accounts, regardless of amount, since they often indicate higher-capacity donors. Likewise, donors who give at any level consistently over time are prime planned giving prospects. Longevity is a promising clue so obvious it doesn't take Holmesian detection skills to suss out.

Dirk Kastra, executive director of the athletics foundation at the University of Virginia, told the *Chronicle of Higher Education* that UVA's development team is focusing extra attention on donors in the $500 to $2,500 annually range—folks who might have been treated, shall we say, cavalierly in the past. Kastra explained, "We think it's an important group of people. They're the leadership gift-givers of tomorrow and major gift donors we might not get to know otherwise."[2]

Kastra is absolutely right. But it's amazing how often such donors are ignored. A recent study conducted by a firm called NextAfter returned astonishing results. NextAfter gave gifts ranging from $1,000 to $5,000 to 37 different groups. Pretty generous contributions, right? Yet only 8 percent of the recipients called to say thanks. Half sent nothing whatsoever in response![3] The NextAfter findings are shocking, yet entirely believable. Even larger gifts often go unrecognized. One of our colleagues had a boss who made a $10,000 gift to an organization he was really excited about. Days, weeks, months went by. He never heard from them. They cashed the check all right, but they couldn't be bothered to drop a single line of thanks.

All donors, no matter the size of their gift, deserve recognition. The form this takes depends upon the level of their support and the resources of the organization.

The most common means of communicating your thankfulness and inviting donors further into the life of your nonprofit are:

PHONE CALLS

Calling a new donor is an excellent way to welcome him or her into your community. It is personal and should be authentic: a genuine expression of gratitude. Phone calls are also a great way to learn more about a donor: about her interests, why she gives to you, and what she hopes to achieve. Some will be laconic or tight-lipped, perhaps nervous in speaking to a stranger, but others will be positively garrulous, only too happy to share opinions or stories or background. (A few, of course, will be rather too happy to share, at interminable length, but these chronic gassers, too, shall pass.) The CEO, development director, or other appropriate staff member can make the call, the details of which should be recorded in your database.

For major gifts—a university with which we work sets the bar at $5,000, though it can be as low as $50, depending upon the size of your organization and number of donors—the president or a development officer calls the donor within 72 hours. (The ideal number of actively managed supporters for a major gifts officer is 50–100; anything higher and donors start slipping through the cracks.)

A thank-you call not only expresses genuine gratitude; it also serves to draw the donor into the life of your organization. Your major gifts officer should use the occasion of a phone call to ask questions, in a casual and entirely non-interrogative way: "What about our letter appealed to you?" "What issues or causes most engage you?" "What motivates your charitable giving?" "Is there a particular way you prefer to be contacted?"

Most people like talking about themselves; give them the opportunity.

This is not to say that pitfalls don't occasionally present themselves. A development officer for a politically oriented magazine tells us that he recently called a new donor to thank him; the man's wife answered, and upon learning of the reason for the call she exclaimed, "He gave to *what?*"

LETTERS OF GRATITUDE (AND TAX RECEIPT LETTERS)

Every donor, even those whom you call, should receive at the very least a personalized form letter of gratitude. It should address the donor by name, not Dear Donor or Dear Friend. The letter must be timely, and it should acknowledge the specific gift by amount and, if applicable, the particular program it is supporting. The letter should go beyond a simple thank-you. You needn't be longwinded about it, but this is an opportunity to let a new donor know more about your organization and establish the fundament of a relationship with him. You should include a business card and direct phone number and email address. Unless volume precludes it, a real person should sign the letter. These details should be recorded in your database. In the case of higher-dollar donors or planned-giving prospects, add a handwritten notecard to the package. In an age of digital communication, this time-honored courtesy can really help you stand out from the crowd.

EMAILS

Emails are fine as an adjunct to phone calls and letters of gratitude, but in no wise are they sufficient as a substitute, except in instances when the gift is made online and no physical address is available. They are at best supplementary.

Don't overdo emails. Yes, they're easy, and they don't require those pesky stamps and envelopes, but they have an evanescent quality. They're too insubstantial; they can be disposed of with the click of a button. That's not to say they are useless: A meaningful, personal email—not a mass emailing from a particular person (not a generic organization address) can leave a good impression. Take care, though, to keep your donor's habits and preferences in mind. While email may be an acceptable method of communication with younger donors, it may not be a good option for older ones.

PREMIUMS, ENCLOSURES, WELCOME PACKAGES, AND SURVEYS

Should you include a gift, premium, or organization materials in your letter of gratitude?

It depends. These can be a nice touch when (1) they are related to the mission of your organization; (2) they are not overwhelming; and/or (3) they were promised in the solicitation (e.g., "For a gift of $100 or more we'll send you a copy of our CEO's latest book"). Some organizations have special "welcome packets" for first-time donors; these provide information about the organization's mission, programs, and what donations help support.

Typically these packets include a welcome letter, a brochure or buck slip insert, and perhaps a gewgaw (doubling as an advertisement) such as a bumper sticker or refrigerator magnet. Don't underestimate the subtle influence of the latter: The donor sees it every time she opens the fridge door to grab a carton of milk or piece of cold pizza, and odds are it is attaching a photo of a child or grandchild or beloved dog to the door. The associative powers are considerable.

Some nonprofits include new donor surveys in these packets. These ask the recipient where his or her interests lie and can be helpful in the tailoring of future communications. New donor surveys should be short and to the point and easy to complete. Don't send a complicated five-page form that conjures up primordial final-exam anxieties. Your goal is to genuinely understand the donor's interests and preferences, not to torment the poor fellow with an arduous interrogation. He is now your partner, and you want to keep it that way.

■ ■ ■

The following is no set of hard-and-fast rules but rather a general and eminently tweakable outline:

Sample First-Time Donor Thank-You Procedure

$1–$99

- ◆ Within a week, a member of your stewardship team— that is, a staffer who is assigned to the care and maintenance of supporters—sends a one-page thank-you form letter from the president (with a high-quality digital or actual hand signature) addressed personally to the donor.

◆ If the volume of work permits, the stewardship team member calls and thanks the donor.

$100–$499

◆ Within a week, the stewardship team member calls the donor and also sends a hand-signed form letter from the president. If necessary, the letter can be signed by the team member on the president's behalf, but really, unless the office is flooded with large donations (and what a pleasant problem that is) the president ought to make time for a weekly letter-signing session.

◆ Within two weeks, assign a contractor or in-house staffer to research the net worth and giving capacity of all $100+ donors. Request a meeting with high-capacity donors. (We'll take up donor research in Chapter 7.)

$500–$999

◆ Within 72 hours, the stewardship team member or—preferably—a senior staffer (major gifts officer, development director, or vice president of marketing) calls to thank the donor.

◆ Within two weeks, perform the aforementioned research and request a meeting with high-capacity donors.

◆ Within two weeks, a senior staffer hand-signs a personalized thank you note (utilizing research) with a handwritten PS.

$1,000–$5,000

◆ Within one week, perform the aforementioned research and request a meeting with high-capacity donors.

◆ Within 24–48 hours, a senior staffer calls the donor.

- Within 24–48 hours, a senior staffer hand-signs a personalized thank-you letter (utilizing research, if possible) with a handwritten PS.

$5,000+
- High-fives all around, happy dances permitted, and the clumsiness of those with two left feet is overlooked.
- Within one week, perform the aforementioned research.
- Within 24–48 hours, the president calls the donor.
- Within 24–48 hours, the president hand-signs a personalized thank-you letter (utilizing research, if possible) with a handwritten PS.

Miscellaneous
- All first-time donors should receive a basic welcome package in a 9×12 envelope accompanying their thank-you note. The welcome package should include one or two pieces of high-quality collateral material (such as a prospectus, a brochure, an annual report, etc.). You might also include a useful and unobtrusive insert—a pen, sticker, bookmark, magnet, or suchlike featuring the organization's name.
- First-time donor thank-you notes should specifically address the recipient as a first-time donor and reference the enclosed materials.
- If the donation level entitles the new donor to any donor club benefits, either include those in the welcome package or mention when the donor can expect to receive them. Special club stationery should be used for these letters, if possible.

House-File Solicitations

Okay, you've thanked donors large and small for their initial gifts. Now you cultivate them with *house-file* letters.

The house-file mailing is a way of bringing donors into the life of your organization without adding staff. It allows you to ingrain your nonprofit and its message in the mind of your donors. Think of these letters as exercises in periodic inculcation.

As with prospecting letters, repetition is your friend! You're not introducing the organization, but you should not assume that the recipient has an insider's knowledge of your activities. Reiterate the mission. Then re-reiterate it. "Re-husk" it, as those from the corn-belt might say. While the tone can be somewhat more casual than that of the prospecting letter, don't forget that the purpose of this epistle is to raise money. Ask on the first page, or at the top of the second at the latest. Thank recipients for their previous support and tell them that their continued patronage will enable you to carry out your mission to even greater effect. Don't worry about the level of detail; you're painting the big picture. Details matter only insofar as they illustrate or lend credibility to your stories. The house-file letter can be shorter than a prospecting letter, as you don't need the same volume of introductory material.

Avoid nuts-and-bolts talk. One of the worst house files we've seen was from a fine organization whose communications were distinguished, in most cases, by a felicity of style. This letter, although well-written, explained at length how a donation would make possible an expanded direct-mail campaign, which in turn would bring new donors and new supporters to the cause. All true—but also (1) boring; and (2) a turn-off. When most people give to a favored nonprofit, they like to think their gift is being used to further the mission of the nonprofit—to comfort the sick, to buy new books for the library, to endow research, to illuminate or promote some political or philosophical position, to purchase new reeds for the woodwinds, or whatever. They do not envision their gift being used for a direct-mail campaign. This pitch might work with a foundation or a particularly enlightened major donor, but not most supporters.

Generally speaking, you should send a minimum of four house-file solicitation letters a year, as well as perhaps two soft asks with a reply card. A soft ask can be the sharing of information, perhaps through a biannual or quarterly newsletter. You want your donors to feel as if they are part of your group; give them the inside scoop on what you're up to. (Well, not *too* inside: "Jenny the research associate has broken up with Ted in accounting; acrimony and recriminations fly" is best kept out of a newsletter, as are "Marvin in the mailroom is hitting the sauce again" and "Marianne the assistant vice president is looking for love in all the wrong places.")

Twelve is the absolute maximum of hard asks per year, though we recommend against this unless your nonprofit is a giant. Getting dunned every month is annoying; 12, or even 8, hard-ask house files a year risks turning your envelopes into circular file dwellers.

To whom do you send house-file solicitations? Surely your list must consist of more than just those who have donated within the last six months, but how far back do you go: Two years? Three years? Five years? Forever?

We advise sending house files to those who have donated sometime within the last 18 months at the least, and three years at the most. For your end-of-the-year appeal you might even go back five years. But don't just dump the others on the list into the fiery pit of the forgotten. Put them in the prospect file; try them again.

Attrition is an unavoidable fact. No matter how strong your program is, you will lose donors. Some people will stop giving, for whatever reason. But err on the side of keeping them on your list; keep them in the loop. Lost sheep do return.

Always ask for specific amounts in these letters. Suggest a donation of two times, 1.5 times, or the same amount as their previous contribution, or perhaps even their *highest* previous contribution, so long as it was not an astronomical outlier. (Though of course you'll happily accept any sum, greater or smaller.)

It is not possible to overstate the importance of regular house-file mailings. Respondents to the most recent American Philanthropic survey solicited their house file an average of nearly five times a year, with average annual solicitation mailings ranging from 3 for organizations with revenue between $100,000 and $499,000 to 7.7 for those with annual revenue of $10 million or above. Response rates were remarkably high, averaging 10.4 percent across all participants.

House files aren't a license to print money, but there are very few fundraising activities that show a better return on investment. The figures from our survey are impressive:

Mean House-File Return on Cost, by Organizational Size

$100K–$499K: 943%

$500K–$999K: 606%

$1M–$2.99: 750%

$3M–$9.99M: 758%

Mean House-File Solicitation Gift Size, by Organizational Size

$100K–$499K: $213

$500K–$999K: $231

$1M–$2.99M: $129

$3M–$9.99M: $163

As you can see, eschewing regular house-file mailings is madness. An average return on cost of between 600 and

900 percent is simply enormous. If you are not currently getting a return somewhere near the lower end of that range, then you may be doing something wrong.

One of our clients, a venerable and well-known magazine run by a nonprofit, had a wide donor base and a deep million-dollar-sized hole in its budget. They were sending out two house-file solicitations a year, raising about half a million per effort, or 10 times their cost. Yet the magazine struggled, as magazines of ideas and culture often do. The situation was close to dire; they were having a hard time meeting payroll. They came to us. What did we do?

We examined their books, vetted their fundraising practices, and came up with a solution of exquisite simplicity. Our brilliant advice: Do a third letter!

If your biannual direct mail is sending forth gushers that would make Jed Clampett sit up and take notice, why not make it *tri*annual? If something works, do it more often!

They did—and that third mailing was every bit as successful as the other two. Then they did a fourth: same result. The budget hole was filled.

The obvious lesson: If you're getting good returns on house-file letters, add another, and maybe another. See how many you can send until the returns decline.

Can you go to the well too often? There's only one way to find out: Do it! When you hit a point of diminishing returns, perhaps with the fourth or fifth or sixth letter, then draw back. But till then, keep dropping the house-file bucket down that well.

SAMPLE HOUSE-FILE DONOR THANK-YOU PROCEDURE

$1–$99

◆ Within a week, a stewardship team member sends a one-page thank-you form letter from the president (with a high-quality digital or actual hand signature) addressed personally to the donor.

$100–$499

◆ Within a week, work volume permitting, a steward-ship team member calls the donor.

◆ Within two weeks, a stewardship team member sends a hand-signed thank-you form letter from the president (signed on his behalf by the team member) or from the team member.

◆ Within four weeks, assign a contractor or in-house staffer to research the net worth and giving capacity of all $100+ donors if not previously researched. Request a meeting with high-capacity donors.

$500–$999

◆ Within a week, a stewardship team member calls the donor.

◆ Within two weeks, a contractor or in-house staffer researches the donor's net worth and giving capacity if not previously researched.

◆ Within two weeks, a stewardship team member sends and hand-signs a personalized thank-you note (utiliz-ing research) with a handwritten PS.

$1,000–$9,999

◆ Within one week, perform the aforementioned research, if not previously undertaken.

◆ Within 72 hours, a senior staffer calls the donor.

◆ Within one week, a senior staffer hand-signs a per-sonalized thank-you letter (utilizing research) with a handwritten PS and requests a meeting, if appropriate. In general, one meeting a year with $1,000+ donors is sufficient, unless the donor seems to require more, in which case meet his meeting needs within reason.

$10,000+

◆ Within one week, perform the aforementioned research, if not previously undertaken.

- Within 24–48 hours, the president calls the donor.
- Within one week, the president hand-signs a personalized thank-you letter (utilizing research) with a handwritten PS and a request for a meeting, if appropriate.

Miscellaneous

- House-file donor thank-you letters should be audience appropriate—that is, they are specifically directed at those who have given before and who have at least a rudimentary knowledge of the organization.
- If the donation level entitles the house-file donor to any donor club benefits, either include them with the thank-you letter or mention when the donor can expect to receive them. Once again, special club stationery should be used for these letters, if possible.
- Board members can also be used to good effect in thanking major donors.

Keep in Mind

- Donations that come in through the website should receive an automatically generated thank-you form email under the President's name, bearing his or her digital signature. Online donations should receive the same treatment as outlined above.
- Send end-of-year tax form letters to each donor as needed, tallying the recipient's contributions during the tax year and thanking him or her. Hand-sign letters to those whose contributions have totaled $1,000 or more and include personalized postscripts.
- These procedures can be adjusted based on volume of work and staff capacity, though always err on the side of a personal (rather than impersonal) touch.
- Those who give planned gifts (confirmed and received) of any amount should be treated with the highest level of attention and courtesy; those who inquire about

planned giving opportunities should receive treatment only a notch below.

♦ Some organizations single out new donors for a special set of communications during the first two months after a gift. The assumption is that the extra attention pays off in increased donor retention. These communications include multiple thank-you notes, newsletters and updates, and pertinent articles or essays. Once the two months are up, the donors are placed into the house-file pool and contacted at the regular frequency. If you have the capability, this is absolutely worth testing.

Lapsed Donors

Let's get back to those lost sheep.

Chances are that you've lost a donor at some point in your organization's history. Actually, it's more a dead certainty than it is a chance. More likely, you've lost dozens, hundreds, or even thousands, depending upon your size.

Donor attrition is a death-and-taxes fact in the fundraising world. Even the most successful nonprofits count on losing donors, though of course they try to reduce attrition and minimize its effect. Organizations typically lose about 40 percent of their donors each year, which is as frustrating as it is unavoidable.

So what do you do with these lapsed givers: Consign them to an outer circle of hell? Vow never to speak their blasted names again? Curse them, their posterity, and the horse they rode in on?

These may be your first instincts, but take a deep breath. What once was lost can now be found, as the hymn goes. Lapsed donors are a source of hidden potential. Herewith are five steps for winning them back:

1. *Know who your lapsed donors are.* You need a database of donor records, and the information in your system must be accurate. This sounds elementary, but it's painful to see how frequently organizations struggle with recordkeeping that is sloppy, fragmentary, and self-defeating. As long as you have donors' contact information and complete giving history (including the amounts, sources, and dates of each gift), you have what you need. Ideally, you can also sort by type: individuals, foundations, and perhaps corporations.

2. *Rank which lapsed donors are most likely to give again.* Run the famous LYBUNT ("Last Year But Unfortunately Not This") report to glean from your database a list of your most recent lapsed donors. These lost sheep are the easiest to return to the fold, especially with end-of-year solicitations. For those whose names don't come up in the LYBUNT query, look for indicators such as frequency of giving, longevity of giving, and gift size. Assign staff to approach the most promising of these individuals and foundations.

3. *Target your communications with lapsed donors.* Distinguish between lapsed and active donors. Acknowledge their past support, share new developments, and ask them to renew. You'll find that in some cases their failure to give is a mere oversight; once reminded, they'll rejoin the ranks of your supporters.

4. *Give your lapsed donors a chance—don't talk yourself out of it before you even try.* Most organizations have a closetful of lost grants and major gifts, and for every one of these lost opportunities there's an explanation: We missed that deadline. The project didn't turn out the way the donor had hoped. We had a falling out at the 2015 gala. Our contact at that foundation left.

Our director of development fostered that relationship and now she's gone . . . . Donors stop giving for many reasons, and sometimes, let's face it, it's our fault. Don't let that be an excuse. Reconnect, send updates, restore or build new relationships; nothing ventured, nothing gained.

5. *Keep track of the lost donors you reacquire.* Just as it's a wise practice to review how many new donors you're acquiring each year, so is it advisable to assess how many lapsed donors you are reacquiring and how you're doing it: By mailings? Personal contact? The cost of reacquiring a lapsed donor is far less than the cost of acquiring a new donor, which is all the more reason to celebrate the return of one who was lost.

In the Twilight of the Year . . .

The days will grow shorter, the nights longer and colder, and the nonprofit fundraiser's thoughts will turn to the year-end mailing to your house file!

There's something askew about planning for Christmas in September, the month when football kicks off, apples are pressed into cider, and the leaves begin to turn, but hey, if Irving Berlin can write "White Christmas" from the point of view of a sun-drenched Beverly Hillsian, you can begin working on your end-of-year house-file letter in September.

Nonprofits rake in a hugely disproportionate share of revenue in the calendar's last quarter: anywhere from 30 to 60 percent, depending upon the source. This fact is well-known in the fundraising world, so you won't have the field to yourself: Every savvy nonprofit will be competing for attention and the attendant dollars as the snow starts to fly up north.

We have found that the most effective model for end-of-year fundraising gathers snail mail, email, social media, and one's website around a unified theme that inspires donors and draws them, from various angles, deeper into the life of your organization.

Step-by-step, month-by-month, the campaign proceeds:

September: Make a Plan

◆ Review last year's results—what you did, what worked and what didn't work—and set your goals for this year.

◆ Develop a theme and narrative—a story arc—for the campaign. Make it as compelling as possible. With your design team, develop a way to convey this theme visually.

◆ Sound out your most stalwart donors to find if one will put up the money for a matching gift (i.e., "A dear friend of ours has offered to match every dollar we receive up to a total of $X").

◆ Draw up an October–January timeline that outlines and assigns all tasks and schedules mailing dates for all communications.

October: Prepare Your End-of-Year Campaign

◆ Engage your audience before the campaign with non-solicitation communications throughout the fall. Get them thinking of you before the Big Ask.

◆ Review the design and functionality—or lack thereof—of your online donation page. Few things annoy potential donors more than unnecessary roadblocks between them and the act of donating.

◆ Review your thank-you and follow-up procedures. Pre-plan promptitude and politeness!

◆ Consider non-solicitation holiday greetings in digital and/or print form. Thanksgiving is the perfect time to thank those whose generosity makes your work possible. This might make your end-of-year ask seem less mercenary.

◆ Draft and develop all print and digital content. Coordinate with the printer and web developer as needed.

November and December: Launch and Sustain Your Campaign

◆ Use email and social media to take advantage of Giving Tuesday, which occurs on the Tuesday after Thanksgiving and advertises itself as the "kickoff of the charitable season." (See givingtuesday.org for more information and resources.)

◆ Mail your house-file end-of-year ask one to three weeks (depending upon the class of postage used) prior to Thanksgiving so as to hit donors' mailboxes no later than early December. Consider a shorter follow-up mailing in mid-December.

◆ Make a major digital push in the last two weeks of December. This should include the following components:
  • 4–8 emails
  • Lightbox or house ads on the website, as applicable
  • Campaign-specific social media postings every day
  • Online advertisements (including paid/promoted content on social media) as applicable
  • At least one post-campaign report and thank-you email, as well as social media updates

January: Measure Your Results and Follow Up

◆ Make sure that your thank-you procedures are firing on all cylinders.

◆ Consider a quick follow-up direct mail and/or email solicitation in mid-January to catch people who lost your pitch in the Christmas blizzard or intended to donate but never quite got around to it. You needn't irritate givers with a letter perceived as pestering; tell them, "If you gave at the end of the year, thank you, and our apologies for this letter; if you didn't get the chance to make an end-of-year donation, I invite you to do so now."

◆ Analyze the campaign and its performance. Start thinking about next year.

◆ Consider convening a small focus group of donors or doing a select survey early in the New Year to get feedback on the campaign.

Finally, remember to start small. You can't do everything, but don't do nothing. Introduce a new element each year. Be agile; if something's not working, adjust. It's important to have a plan and stick to it, but leave room for creativity and spontaneity; slavish adherence to a rigid formula is how duds are born.

■ ■ ■

Okay, so you've prospected as vigorously as Yukon Cornelius, you've thanked givers with a fulsomeness that would shame Liberace, and you've moved your new donors into a nice roomy house file. Now it's time to shave in all the necessary places, dress to the nines (or at least tuck in your shirt and brush the knots out of your hair), and take those meetings!

ENDNOTES

1. Steven Shattuck, "Why Small Donations Should Matter a Lot to Nonprofits," *Bloomerang*, June 10, 2017, https://bloomerang .co/blog/why-small-donations-matter-and-how-nonprofits-should-handle-them/.

2. Brad Wolverton and Sandhya Kambhampati, "Colleges Raised $1.2 Billion in Donations for Sports in 2015," *Chronicle of Higher Education*, accessed January 29, 2016, https://www.chronicle.com/article/Colleges-Raised-12-Billion/235058.

3. *The Mid-level Donor Crisis: What We Learned from Donating $1000 or More to 37 Different Organizations* (Plano, TX: Next After, 2015), https://www.nextafter.com/mid-level-donor-crisis/. The entire Next After study is free and well worth reading.

Chapter 6

Getting to Know You: Meetings, Donor Clubs, and Planned Giving

We have a saying at American Philanthropic: Nothing works like a meeting. (Apologies to John Deere.) The single best use of a nonprofit leader's time is to meet with her donors.

Aside from your family, how have you forged the most enduring and rewarding relationships of your life? By spending time with people, sharing a meal, a drink, a ballgame, a concert, a prayer group—any face-to-face experience. That's what builds bonds. And that is exactly what you are trying to do—or *ought* to be trying to do—with your supporters.

Personal meetings are the essential cultivation tool, with the emphasis on *personal*. So how do you prepare? What do you need to know before you head off to meet with that $1,000 donor whom you would like to ultimately become a $10,000 donor?

First, you'll want to do your research. Know the person's giving patterns and giving capacity so that your ask will be reasonable: not too high and not too low, in Three Little Bears fashion. (Though it is always better to ask for too much than too little, unless the "too much" is outrageously high.) Go into the meeting with a high and low ask in mind, but trust your perceptions. Be sensitive to hints. If you're talking to Debbie Downer and she's whining about a stock market freefall or how she had to cut out the Christmas trip to Aspen this year, adjust the high and low asks accordingly.

Prepare but don't be preprogrammed; your aim is to make a personal connection with the donor. Go to listen; get to know her. What motivates her? What is she interested in? Why is she giving you money? Know your stuff and be ready to answer questions, but don't be surprised if the queries are elementary and sparse. It is shocking how little many donors know, and often care, about your program. Some may want specific information, but most will not. More likely, if things are going well, they'll just ask, "How can I help? What do you need?" Have answers to these questions at the ready.

135

Always convey passion and enthusiasm for your mission. These are infectious; so, alas, is their absence. If you or your development officer come off as bored, distracted, indifferent, or just going through the motions, you're going to return empty-handed, and deservedly so. Yes, these meetings can be a routine, but there is joy even in the regular, the everyday, the commonplace. Find it; share it. And if you can't, find someone else to make these calls.

Don't be diffident about asking for money. This isn't like working up the nerve to ask Uncle Clem for ten grand to pay off gambling debts. The request isn't coming out of nowhere; wealthy people understand that the intention of the meeting is a petition for funds.

How do you set up donor meetings? For prospects, we preach letters first. (If the donor is in your house file, just go ahead and call.) Send the letter via Priority Mail. Now, if you use Federal Express, we can guarantee the envelope will be opened. No one in history has ever thrown away a Fed-Ex package. (Well, maybe Rick James or Lindsay Lohan in a bad moment, but they're not giving to you, anyway.) Very few people have ever thrown away a Priority Mail package, either, and it's $25 cheaper than Fed-Ex. Moreover, Federal Express can seem last-minute or hurried, even desperate. And it strikes the frugal—including frugal rich guys—as wasteful.

(Parenthetically, a friend tells us of a major Washington think-tank that shipped urgent overnight appeals to big donors via UPS. Unfortunately, one target of this mailing was the CEO of Federal Express. You can bet that some poor intern or secretary was scapegoated for that one.)

So send the Priority Mail letter requesting a meeting. Don't say you're only coming to town if they say yes; people recoil from that. It lades the meeting with too many expectations. Instead, tell them that you'll be in town, say, May 10–15, and that you'd love to see them.

You probably won't get an immediate return call (or Priority Mail package). That's okay. Call to tell them that you're just following up on the letter. In fact, the letter rarely works on its own, so don't expect it to; it's really just an excuse to make the call.

And if you get no response? With a prospect, try twice, three times at most. Then move on, reserving the possibility of circling back at a later date.

People appreciate being asked, being remembered. They like being invited to things, too, even if they don't attend. A supporter from California probably isn't going to fly to Virginia for a half-day seminar or event, but it doesn't hurt to extend the invitation. Keep in touch with your donors; don't just come out of the woodwork when you're asking them for money.

Since we can't say it enough, we'll say it one more time. *Relationship-building is crucial.* And with your larger donors, meeting face-to-face is essential to forging that relationship.

Our first American Philanthropic survey produced some fascinating results in this realm—some of them counterintuitive. In the dog-bites-man category of the fully expected, representatives of large organizations conducted significantly more meetings than did those from smaller groups:

Mean Number of Donors and Prospects Met with per Year, by Organizational Size
Average: 106.9

$100K–$499K: 22.9

$500K–$999K: 64.3

$1M–$2.99M: 87.8

$3M–$9.99M: 176.7

$10M+: 581.1

Mean Number of Donor/Prospect Meetings per Development Staffer, by Organizational Size
Average: 36.2

$100K–$499K: 17.8

$500K–$999K: 54.7

$1M–$2.99M: 32.2

$3M–$9.99M: 36.4

$10M+: 75.0

Mean Number of Meetings per Development Staffer, by Organizational Effectiveness
Highly Effective Organizations: 40.6

Other Organizations: 34.1

And now for the man-bites-dog finding:

Mean Percentage of Meetings That Are Asks, by Organizational Effectiveness
Highly Effective Organizations: 39.5%

Other Organizations: 51.1%

This is really striking. Less than 40 percent of the meetings taken by representatives of highly effective organizations are asks while more than half of those conducted by the other organizations include a request for funds. These non-ask meetings are investments in relationship-building, and also in—we write this without a trace of cynicism—friendship.

Yes, friendship. Unless your motives are purely mercenary, in which case it is exceedingly improbable that you are reading this book, you are likely to develop a friendship, or at least warm acquaintanceship, with donors with whom you meet on multiple occasions. You are, after all, comrades united in a common cause and thus bound by something stronger than a mere cash nexus.

Take the Meeting—Please

Occasionally one of our more aloof, diffident, or socially awkward clients will tell us, "I don't need to meet with people if I can just show them a good return on investment." However ardently they may wish this were so, it is arrantly, self-destructively, untrue.

All the good work your nonprofit is doing will be for naught if you don't cultivate your donors. An example:

A client of ours, a prestigious faith-based publication, was left with a substantial nest egg when its founder died. His replacement as editor and CEO was a talented poet. *Ah*, we see you cringing. We know what you're thinking—the poet must have been a woolgathering dreamer who squandered the nest egg, spending dollars as freely as a stream-of-consciousness versifier spends words. Well, that's not exactly the case. And besides, the ranks of top-flight poets include such successful businessmen as Wallace Stevens, Dana Gioia, and Ted Kooser.

The poet reconceptualized the magazine, and he didn't do a bad job of it. But—here the stereotype claims another victim—he was not a numbers guy. He was almost an anti-numbers guy. He had a vision but no interest in raising money. That was the province of less ethereal souls. Their task in this life was to amass, and his was to spend. Perhaps in some alternative universe this division of labor obtains, but in the here-and-now the editor and CEO of a small magazine has to raise money. If he doesn't, the magazine ceases to exist.

So the board of directors canned the poet and hired a theologian. This might seem like a lateral move, in a hard-headed business sense—rather like withdrawing your nomination of Seth Rogen as *People Magazine*'s "Sexiest Man Alive" and substituting Steve Buscemi—but the theologian did not share the poet's disdain for fundraising. When he discovered, upon assuming his position, just how bad a shape the magazine was in, he came to us.

"I don't know how to raise money," he told us. "Tell me what to do."

We did. The theologian proved remarkably disciplined. Each week we gave him a list of the high-dollar donors with whom he needed to speak. He did so. If you hit your goals at the $1,000 level, you're fine, because adding and renewing $1,000 donors at a good clip means that your letters of gratitude are working, your house file is working, and your cultivation is working. Tracking $1,000 donors can be an important metric on which to focus, so the theologian spent one day a week (not Sunday!) cultivating them.

He kept his eyes on the prize. He looked to move his $1,000 contributors up to $5,000, and his $5,000 up to $10,000. If he had to fly to California on business, or even pleasure, he'd ask us for a list of the donors and prospects with whom he should meet. He's an unlikely fundraiser—he's a theologian, for God's sake!—but he's personable, diligent, and effective.

Does he enjoy it? Well, do *you* enjoy asking people for money? Probably not; it's weird to enjoy asking people for money. You should feel uncomfortable. But that's not what fundraising is really about. *Fundraising isn't about asking people for money*. It's about building relationships, and there's nothing weird or unsavory about that.

The theologian also has the wisdom to get out of his own way. Too many CEOs get involved and bogged down in the little things. For instance, a direct-mail letter goes out. A board member receives it. He calls the CEO. "There's a misplaced comma in this letter!" the punctilious (or pedantic) board member hollers. A punctuation error: the horror!

The CEO blows his top. Why is the board member receiving a house-file letter? And who misplaced the comma? This is unacceptable! From now on, he rages, I need to see every letter before it goes out. I'll draft the darned letter myself. And I must also see every name on the house-file list before it goes out.

This gums up the process. It takes the CEO/president's eye off what he should be focusing on. It detours him into a bog that will sap his energy to no good purpose.

Sometimes these little blowups occur because a direct-mail vendor is sending out letters that don't exactly fill organizational hearts with pride. In fact, they're downright embarrassing. If this is the case, cut the vendor loose. Offensive or stupid letters are not worthy of you; culturally, they are poison. They contribute, in their small but real way, to the degradation of American discourse. Everyone in your organization, from small donors to staff to major donors and board members, should be proud of your direct mail. It should never say anything that isn't true.

At opposite poles from the diligent theologian was a nonprofit CEO who was asocial even for an economist. He helmed a small politically oriented think-tank that ought to have been rolling in dough, given the populist passion ignited by his central issue. Alas, he gave nerds a bad name.

"I'm terrible at small-talk," he told us. "I can't go into an old lady's living room and have tea and scones and talk about the weather." So he recognized his deficiency, but he refused to do anything about it. We weren't asking him to undergo a gregariousness transplant, but rudimentary people skills ought not to have been beyond his grasp. He had no development officer—this was a promising startup, but it hadn't achieved liftoff yet, so there were but two employees. Besides, donors want to hear from the boss, not a subaltern. Plenty of our clients would prefer to farm out fundraising to others in the office, but even in outfits with large development staffs, donors—particularly major ones—want to meet the head honcho. They want to talk with him or her. They need that personal connection.

Well, we'd introduce this CEO to people and they were almost immediately repelled. Indeed, one president of a large manufactory whose product was related to this CEO's specialty and who routinely gave seven-figure gifts to kindred organizations requested a meeting with him, which is the equivalent of saying, "I want to give you money. How much do you need?" They met—and the manufacturer's check-signing pen never left his pocket. The economist-CEO had missed the layup and failed to hit the ball off the tee. He had actually talked a willing and eager and very rich giver out of a gift.

It's one thing to be shy—most of us are, and a certain modesty can be quite winning—but it's another to be rude or a cipher. At last check, the economist who ought to have been rolling in dough was still half-baked.

If your president or CEO is hopelessly slothful or offensive—and if your shop hasn't closed doors yet—send a development officer instead. The important thing is the meeting. Sending *someone*, even a junior staffer, is better than no one.

Another CEO, this one a reserved academic, actually blew off three foundation meetings because he didn't want to go through the trouble of changing an Amtrak ticket. It was too big an inconvenience. That train, you can bet, left the station (probably an hour late, given that it was Amtrak).

Incredibly, though, it came back. A year later we secured him a second-chance meeting with one of those foundations. The train was on time and he actually showed up. He called one of our associates immediately after. "It was a disaster," he sulked, "an utter failure." The foundation staffers were "weird." They fell asleep during his presentation. They asked pointed questions dipped in hostility. It was a complete waste of his time, he told us angrily.

Several weeks later, the foundation awarded the academic's nonprofit a $30,000 grant—more than had been requested.

When people meet, good things happen. CEOs who are willing to roll up their sleeves and meet with donors, build relationships, put in the time, and make the investment will succeed. Those unwilling to do so, those forever delegating and being derelict in their duty, will fail.

Even those who don't like it—even the shy, the timid, the haughty, the socially clumsy—must do it or their organizations will die. One CEO, an awkward fellow whom no one has ever called convivial, was aware of his personal limitations yet found ways to work around them. For instance, when house files went out he asked for a stack of his top 100 donors and he wrote little notes at the top of each letter. A small touch that costs nothing but time—and believe us, *it makes a difference.*

An energetic CEO can even redress the errors of his predecessors. When a young, charismatic fellow took the helm at a policy organization in the Deep South, he found a board of directors that was thoroughly disengaged, even ignorant of the entity's function. They were friends of the previous CEO and served only as amiable rubberstamps for their buddy. When the crony-collector left, his successor quickly apprehended the fix he was in. So he set out to build relationships, meeting with each member of the board, explaining the mission of the organization, the details of which came as news to the heretofore unenlightened board members. He also recruited new directors who were aligned with him personally and the organization philosophically. He made sure to send regular updates on their work; he built a loop and kept the directors in it. Today the organization thrives.

Amazing things happen when you meet with people. Five-hundred-dollar-a-year donors jump up to $7,500; those at the $1,000 level metamorphose into $30,000 givers. (Those numbers aren't plucked from the air: A young, energetic development director with whom we work notched these gifts within a fortnight of this writing.)

Sometimes not even a bumbling boss can screw up a substantial gift. Take a trip back in time with us:

While serving as an executive at a venerable nonprofit focused on educating college students in the principles of ordered liberty, one of us—we'll protect the innocent and call him Blake—receives a phone call from a noted agronomist at the University of California, Davis. The man's academic specialty is large-animal husbandry in Africa—not exactly a matter within the organization's wheelhouse.

No matter: The Afro-agronomist said he had read the organization's flagship journal for 20 years, though he had no prior connection with group. He tells Blake that when his financial planner had suggested he set up a foundation, he responded that there was already an organization that did exactly what he'd do if he had a foundation, so he'd prefer to just give it the gift rather than bothering with all that hassle and red tape.

"How much are we talking?" Blake asks, expecting, perhaps at best, a sum in the low five figures.

"Nine million dollars," the man replies, as casually as if he were reporting the day's temperature.

Alas, a fly sneaks into the ointment. Blake's boss, the CEO, a meddlesome marplot, says that he'd like to meet this mystery benefactor. Blake's heart sinks. Jason, the boss, instructs Blake to set up a meeting with the man, who lives in Spokane. Jason will fly from the East Coast to Seattle, Blake's base, and the two will make the trip across Washington State.

Jason has an idea: Let's give the man a plaque. (Just what he wants! Yes, that's why he's about to give the organization the largest single donation in its history: because he wants it acknowledged with a plaque he can hang in his den!) Jason has a piece of parchment signed by the members of the board, several of whom had been flunkies of varying degrees of prominence in a previous presidential administration. The framed document is then Fex-Exed to Blake in Seattle. Blake is stressing out, awaiting Jason's arrival and babysitting the plaque. Jason calls before he boards the plane. "Blake," he drawls in his honeyed Southern accent, "were you planning on washing your car?"

Not really, but . . .

"I think it'd be awfully nice if we drove up to see Mr. Smith in a clean car."

Now, Mr. Smith does not give a damn if Blake's car is spic'n'span clean or *Grapes of Wrath*–level dirty. *He does not care.* But to Jason, appearance is everything.

Blake and Jason drive the four-and-a-half hours. It is excruciating. They arrive an hour early and park their freshly washed car a couple of blocks away. It's a torrid day; Blake's shirt sticks to his skin; his back is drenched in sweat.

Finally Blake and Jason walk up to Mr. Smith's door. They are both wearing suits, a sartorial edict that Jason had delivered, overruling Blake's suggestion of casual dress. They look like two particularly stiff FBI agents. Jason is carrying the plaque, which is encased in bubble wrap and hidden inside a large bag. Mr. Smith opens the door. He's dressed in a t-shirt and Birkenstocks. After an awkward introduction they sit down to chat. Things get more stilted by the minute. Did we mention that Mr. Smith's wife is dying? So things are funereal as well as awkward.

Jason is fussing with the plaque. Something about it seems off to him: a staple is sticking out. He tries to push it in but instead shatters the glass. It breaks into dozens of pieces. Little shards dapple the carpet. Mr. Smith and his wife look on, if not in horror, then in puzzlement. What, they wonder, are these lunatics doing? Jason kneels and frantically plucks the slivers of glass from the carpet.

"I'm so sorry," he says. "We'll get this plaque reframed and send it to you."

Just what Mr. Smith and his dying wife want to hear!

The visit could hardly have gone worse. Yet it doesn't matter. The organization gets Mr. Smith's $9 million. Not even a clumsy CEO and shattered glass can deter a determined donor.

Donor Clubs

A donor club that includes your major supporters serves two main purposes. First, it recognizes donors and gives you a way of expressing appreciation in a public way, as a supplement to letters and phone calls and personal meetings. Second, these clubs provide an incentive to donors to increase their giving, threshold by threshold, each year.

Linking a request for gifts to a Donor Club softens the ask and invests it with additional purpose. Asking the recipient to join (or renew her membership in) the Sterling Society or Platinum Club is a gussied-up way of soliciting a higher-than-average donation.

Our most recent survey measured nonprofits with active, organizationally important donor clubs against those without such clubs. Groups in the former category raised more than twice as much money on average from their individual donors.

Donor clubs work.

There are five traits of good donor clubs:

1) *They convey prestige and an aura of exclusivity.* Here as elsewhere, little things can make a difference. You want to give members the sense that they are part of the inner circle, the organizational core. You can do this by giving the club a distinct brand, its own aesthetic. Use different stationery than you use for other communications; perhaps a different logo or thicker, heavier paper. The president or whoever signs donor club letters might hand-sign rather than use an e-signature. Whenever you address a member of the donor club, be sure to mention his membership.

2) *They have a mission-specific name and benefits.* Don't just call it the Executive Club or the Inner Circle. Give the club a singular name, not a cookie-cutter moniker that any of a thousand other clubs might use. For instance, *First Things*, the journal of faith and ideas, has an "Editor's Club" presided over by Rusty Reno, its talented editor. Rusty writes the letters in his own inimitable style and frequently travels to stay in personal touch with higher-end donors. Embrace the obscure: The Theology of the Body Institute, named after a central concept of Pope John Paul II's papacy, has the "129 Wednesdays Society," so named because the doctrine is based upon 129 Wednesday talks given by the Pope. A South Carolina think-tank has a Spero Society, a nod to the state motto, *Dum Spiro Spero*, or "While I breathe, I hope." The venerable conservative magazine *National Review* has the "1955 Society" in recognition of the year of its founding.

Benefits accruing to donor club members should be mission-specific. Lapel pins, pens, and the like should bear the name or logo of the organization. They needn't be lavish; these small tokens are not an incentive to join. No one is going to write a check for $5,000 for the promise of a free pen. The incentive is access to you and to the leadership. These folks want to be part of what you are doing; they want to be on your team. Make them feel welcome. For instance, issue an open invitation to lunch with the president when they are in town. Don't worry: You won't be inundated with out-of-town lunch guests. Very few will ever take you up on the offer, but it's nice to be asked.

3) *There should be just one club but it should have multiple levels.* Don't make this labyrinthine. You don't need a plethora of clubs or stratification into 33 separate degrees, à la the Scottish Rite Masons. In fact, we prefer the word *Society*, with its Tocquevillian echoes, to *Club*, which is serviceable but also redolent of climbing into treehouses or golfing. (Not that we have anything against those two excellent pastimes!)

Alumni clubs and opera societies and the like frequently have too many tiers, too many levels. Keep it simple. We recommend the establishment of a single donor club, or society, with perhaps three or four levels, keyed to the size of the donation. The membership floor might be $1,000 in annual donations, for if you're trying to build a healthy, sustainable organization for the long term, these people will be your base. Moreover, a $1,000 donation signals a certain level of affluence. Someone who gives $1,000 can probably give $5,000, maybe $10,000. It's a significant benchmark. The future giving patterns of a $1,000 donor differ from those of a $100 donor, though the goal with a $100 donor is to drive him up to $1,000. Membership in a donor club can be a puissant incentive.

Ideally you'll have enough donors at the $25,000 or $50,000 level to create a higher donor club tier or maybe two, but the $1,000-per-year reliables are your bread-and-butter.

The primary benefit of membership is access: Those at all levels should be invited to special events while the higher levels might be invited to participate in conference calls with the president and/or key staffers. Again, the important thing is to cultivate a sense of belonging, of fellowship and sorority, of being on the same team, pushing toward the same goals.

4) *Benefits should be few and easy to fulfill.* This is not a market transaction. No one is joining your club in exchange for whatever gimcracks you're sending out. Be creative but don't go overboard. Don't delay the launching of your donor club just because you can't decide upon an apt or striking token of thanks for members. You don't even have to be clear at first: There's nothing wrong with advertising a vague "Invitation to Special Events!" as the lure. Nor should you make promises you might not be able to keep (e.g., a pledge to send a monthly newsletter, or a new tchotchke every quarter). Not only are these acts time-consuming, but if you miss a deadline or two and fall behind, you'll be tempted to terminate the club.

Academically or politically oriented nonprofits often offer signed books from the organization's president to club members. Proceed with caution: You don't want to squander too much staff time mailing signed books that no one will read. Instead, tell them that you'll happily send a signed copy of your president's latest book *upon request*. Asking members to opt-in to receive benefits allocates staff time more efficiently and reduces postage costs.

Done right, donor club benefits strengthen the bond between giver and recipient. For instance, colleges sometimes send sketches or photographs of beloved campus buildings or scenes to donors. The Intercollegiate Studies Institute sent major donors belonging to its William F. Buckley Jr. Society jars of Red Wing peanut butter: Mr. Buckley's favorite, and a brand not readily available on the shelf of your local supermarket. This was a real hit. So consumables can work as benefits if the item, the nonprofit, and the mission align, even if elliptically.

Remember: The club exists to recognize donors and affirm their membership, not as an incentive or payoff. A lapel pin, tie, or scarf bearing the emblem of your nonprofit is enough. People really do wear these things; never underestimate the bonding power of garmenture!

Launch the club with a letter welcoming as charter members all donors whose contributions over the past year qualify them for membership. Also invite lower-level donors to increase their gifts to a size sufficient to qualify them for membership in at least the outer rings of your circle. Periodically invite non-member donors to join the club and ask current members to either renew their membership or upgrade to the next level.

Event? *Oy Vey!*

We are less than enthusiastic about cultivating givers with events, especially those that require substantial planning and staff time. Charities tend to overinvest in events, which can be draining for organizations and raise nominal amounts of money, especially when opportunity cost is factored into the fundraising equation. This is not, however, to say they're not worth doing: Our most recent survey found that while revenue from events as a percentage of total development income is vanishingly small for the largest organizations ($10M+: 0.3%), it is nearly 5 percent for small groups ($500K–$999K: 4.8%). There is no difference in this measure between highly effective organizations and the others.

Inevitably, someone—a staffer, a board member, a starstruck donor—will suggest that you bring in a Big Name—a TV or radio personality—to keynote a gala dinner or special event. Smile, thank him for the suggestion, and *don't do it!*

Yes, it sounds exciting, and it appeals to our natural laziness: Who wouldn't rather produce a single lucrative event—with Star Power!—than execute, day in and day out, the essential but admittedly unsexy tasks necessary to effective nonprofit fundraising? This sounds like easy money, but it's not. You'll pay a king's ransom for these celebrities to breeze through, read a canned speech (with YOUR NAME and YOUR CITY inserted at appropriate points), shake a few hands, and decamp. You'll be out their speaking fee, hundreds of staff hours, and quite possibly high opportunity costs in the form of missed direct-mail deadlines, phone calls not made, and thank-you letters not sent.

Case in point: A respected public policy outfit in the Pacific Northwest banked on a controversial radio celebrity attracting thousands of new supporters, who in turn would open their checkbooks and write out numbers with lots of zeroes. They rented a professional baseball stadium, expended a hefty sum on promoting the event, charged a princely $55 per ticket—and no one came. Or, rather, an audience trickled in. The crowd barely filled the infield. If a centerfielder had been patrolling the outfield, he'd have had plenty of room to roam, and in the stands the multitude was evidently disguised as a sea of empty seats.

The result was a huge financial loss, public embarrassment, and virtually no new members. The lesson: no big one-off events! Even if people show, those are not the people who are going to join or contribute to your organization. They are not going to be converted into donors, no matter how large your advertising budget. Mass events that are out of character do not bring in new donors. They are drains on your budget and staff time. Moreover, the people who give you money want to hear from *you*, the CEO, and not a canned speech from the governor or a hired-gun celebrity.

On a related note, do not advertise on national radio or TV programs such as Sean Hannity or Rush Limbaugh (for conservatives) or Rachel Maddow or Chris Hayes (for liberals). It's expensive, and by and large you're not attracting donors who are in it for the long haul.

Of course you can always luck out. The Terry Schiavo Life and Hope Network, named for the Florida woman in a vegetative state who was the subject of a long and contentious fight between her husband and her parents over whether to remove her feeding tube, advertised that radio controversialist Glenn Beck would headline its annual gala a couple of years ago. The cost of paying for Beck to fly in on a private jet was substantial—so substantial as to guarantee that the dinner would lose money, despite brisk ticket sales. In a prime case of lemons producing the most delicious lemonade, Beck canceled the day before, saving the Schiavo charity a huge sum of money, and the gala—packed with people who had bought tickets expecting to see Beck—turned a tidy profit. But unless you can find a celebrity able to come down with a very timely attack of the flu, this stratagem is best eschewed.

If you must put on an event, make it congruent with your mission—so congruent that it seems utterly natural, even inevitable. An ironclad rule repeats itself:

> There is nothing worth doing in development only once.

Don't rent a baseball stadium and invite a radio ranter whom you are paying tens of thousands of dollars to repeat his on-air shtick. An annual dinner in your home city is far better. Do the same people and companies buy tables every year? Excellent! Do it again and again, introducing just enough freshness into each iteration so as to avoid the tedium of the routine.

The worst events—from a fundraising if not a jollity standpoint—are those that have nothing to do with an organization's mission. Case in point: A New England client of ours sponsored a day of shooting and cigar smoking and whiskey drinking at a private club to which one of its board members belonged. (The shooting, we were assured, would come *before* the whiskey drinking.)

The lean organization's three-person staff devoted most of its time for a period of weeks to this event. Hopes were high: A board member had assured them that his wealthy friends would be there, so introductions would be made, connections laid, pricey admissions paid.

The gathering came off well. It was perfectly benign: Fine whiskey was sipped, expensive cigars smoked, witty—well, maybe half-witty—badinage engaged in, but hardly a dollar was raised, because there was no ask. Those gathered had not been informed that this was a fundraiser. This was a purely social event, a chance for those of like mind to come together in fellowship (and understand that a not-inconsiderable number of your female donors will feel uncomfortable at whiskey-and-cigar nights), but even though that whiskey was being sipped and those cigars smoked by men of wealth, precious little of that wealth wound up in the coffers of our client.

We tried to warn them off. Yes, a few deep-pocketed firearm and cigar enthusiasts might be there, but these pastimes had nothing to do with the think-tank's realm of concerns. The affluent stogey-chomping whiskey-swilling marksmen would have a good time, but this would be the equivalent of a one-night stand. They would not become donors. In fact, because the think-tank hadn't billed the event as a fundraiser, the attendees might have been nonplussed if they were hit up while smoking a Montecristo.

All in all, it was a pleasant waste of time—and it cost the organization dearly in squandered staff hours.

Another client had greater success with a dinner cruise from the Chicago Harbor into Lake Michigan. The purpose of the event—the raising of money—was made clear beforehand. The CEO of an allied organization was the main speaker. He was pithy and pointed. I am here, he said in so many words, to sing the praises of this fine outfit and encourage you to donate to them. He spoke for perhaps five minutes, and brevity was not only the soul of wit but also the key to the checkbook. Brachylogy paid. The president of the nonprofit spoke, too, also for five minutes, as did a board member. In a nice touch, a student whose studies had been assisted by the group said a few words of gratitude.

Parenthetically, students are an underutilized resource (or prop, if we can use that word in a non-pejorative sense).

Most older people, which is to say anyone over 35 or 40, like to help or mentor or advise promising or enterprising youths. The young evoke avuncular or auntly feelings in adults. So, ring those chimes. If your organization benefits young people with scholarships or internships, be sure to advertise the more photogenic or appealing of the lot. Adorn your communications with their faces; excerpt their testimony or witness in mailings; encourage them to say a few words at fundraisers or even board meetings. The student who spoke on the Lake Michigan cruise was ideal: young, fresh-faced, eager, likeable . . . exactly the kind of young person his elders enjoy lending a hand. (Of course, if the only youths you can dig up are inarticulate boys wearing inverted baseball caps bill-backwards or girls with prominent and lurid tramp stamps, you might reconsider this strategy. And don't use stock photos; they reek of inauthenticity. Also, don't fabricate stories by bundling disparate students into composites. Keep it real, as the young folks say.)

The best events are those that track closely with your mission. For instance, state-oriented policy groups might sponsor A Day at the Statehouse, at which donors gather in the State Capitol to hear from legislators, analysts, and representatives of your organization.

Bad events are those that have nothing whatsoever to do with your mission. For instance, we had a private school in the Northeastern United States ask us for advice on running a golf tournament in Mexico. All we could do was shake our heads. There are many fine golf courses south of the border, and we are admirers of the country and people of Mexico, but there was not even an attenuated link between the event and the sponsoring institution. A handful of wealthy donors likely would have shown up and had a fine weekend, but the amount of staff time that would go into the planning and execution of a Mexican golf weekend far outweighs the money that would have been raised.

Count us as skeptics, too, of the ever-popular 5K race for [Fill in the Blank]. Sure, you'll get a few bucks from entrants, but they're just there because they like to run. They don't care about your group. They'll pay the entry fee and after the last lap you'll never hear from them again. It's a one time gift, but they don't even think of it as a gift. It's a single-shot transaction. You may wind up holding a list of names and email addresses but they're next to worthless—except as people to invite to your next 5K.

It's like the ice-bucket challenge we discussed earlier. How many who gave to ALS because of the ice-bucket challenge ever gave again? Effectively zero. Taking an arctic water bath has nothing to do with finding a cure for amyotrophic lateral sclerosis, and pounding the pavement for five kilometers has nothing to do with your nonprofit (unless you're running a shin-splint support group).

Along the same lines, though a rather more profitable branch, a gamer with a popular YouTube channel is in the habit, at the end of each show, of asking viewers to send donations to a different charity. The development officer at one such charity came into work one day to find, *mirable dictu*, that his organization's bank account was richer by tens of thousands of dollars—Manna from heaven, and 500 new donors!

The development officer set out to cultivate those 500. Surely this stream would gush greenbacks! Two months later, he had raised a grand total of $30.

So avoid Mexican golf tournaments and 5Ks. If an Internet sensation drops $50,000 in your kitty, be thankful, use it well, but don't expect this to be a gift that keeps on giving. Just keep your eyes on the prize: mail, meetings, foundations; bring in small donors, turn small donors into big donors, build the base, and develop relationships. These are what matter.

■ ■ ■

Eventually, a helpful soul will point out that your nonprofit is having a birthday. Isn't that worth celebrating, perhaps with a glamorous, starstudded, black-tie-and-evening-gown dinner? Shouldn't you throw a party?

Maybe; but only if it doesn't interfere with the fundamentals.

The giant annual gala is the social centerpiece of many a nonprofit's year. Yet we have seen numerous organizations overinvest in such events. Okay, so it's your fifth anniversary: Who cares? The universe of people who want to pay hundreds of dollars to sit and listen to self-congratulatory speechifying and eat indigestible chicken is narrow. If you must celebrate your anniversary—and you probably should, in some form or another—at least showcase the people (kids or students, ideally) whom your work has benefited.

It's not that celebrations and festal dinners are necessarily a waste of money or counterproductive: Bringing donors together, making them feel a part of your organization, is important. But they should not be a priority to the exclusion of more fundamental activities. They cost a lot of money and chew up a lot of staff time: more often than not, too *much* money and too *much* staff time.

Case in point: A client of ours, a very successful nonprofit, throws a large annual gala in its Southern home city. It raises several hundred thousand dollars. This ain't chump change. But it becomes all-consuming. It takes up a huge amount of time.

This client has a smaller-than-advisable development staff. Several years ago Jeremy was meeting with the president, chief development officer, and several underlings. One of the younger staffers mentioned in passing that no thank-you letters—not a single one—had gone out for the past 90 days because of the organizational focus on the gala.

That's three months of gifts—unacknowledged. In the world of the effective nonprofit, this is unforgivable. Thank-yous are critical. And this group never made the same mistake again.

The president of another client, this one based in the Rockies, confessed to one of our associates that he had yet to scan the multiyear development plan we had drawn up for him because he'd been busy for the last four months selling tables for the annual dinner. "Live for Today" is a good pop song, but it's terrible advice for an organization seeking a long life.

Thinking of the letters that didn't go out, the foundation applications missed, the thank-yous inexcusably delayed—it's enough to send a fundraising consultant straight to the overpriced cash bar.

And let's face it: These rubber-chicken repasts are boring as hell. They're stiff, forced, and stupefying. You watch the clock as the speakers drone on and wonder just how early you can leave without seeming rude. Far better to sponsor a cocktail reception at a funky or interesting tavern with one speaker—humorous and compelling—a cash bar, hors d'oeuvres, and lively chatter. The opportunity costs are minimal, connections are made or deepened, your direct mail stays on schedule, and a fine time is had by all.

Properly scaled events can strengthen the ties that bind you to your donors. For instance, a California-based research organization gathers anywhere from 20 to 50 people for regularly scheduled dinners at which they meet, chat with, and hear from institute researchers in an intimate setting. The mix of diners is about half donors and half prospects. Like a formal dinner of old, they are seated alternately, though instead of male–female the pattern is donor–prospect, so some low-key proselytizing goes on between sips of merlot. The dinners bring people together and give them a meaningful experience. Happily, the day after always seems to bring at least one $10,000 gift or an upgrade from a current supporter.

Similarly, the Manhattan Institute, a free-market-oriented think-tank (in New York, not Kansas), hosts frequent lunches at which Institute fellows talk about their recent work to an audience of donors, members of the conservative New York intelligentsia, and the occasional luminary. As with the California dinners, friends and potential friends are made to feel part of something bigger than just themselves; they are part of a movement, a tradition, or, at the least, the elite population of those interested in ideas. The small scale, as well as the smart event design (with a heavy dose of unstructured socializing time and smaller formal program), ensures that people have the chance to talk to one another, to make connections, and not merely to sit passively while a celebrity listlessly lisps out a canned speech to an anonymous audience.

These smaller events build relationships. Their value is in the mingling, the commingling, the gathering together of people who might otherwise feel isolated or alone. You are helping them meet others of like mind and like interests. And you are fortifying your own group, for without relationships of greater solidity than the mere cash nexus, organizations wither and die.

These cultivating events can help you nurture and grow your community. Just don't let them distract you from the necessaries: getting out your direct mail and thank-yous on time, returning calls, meeting with donors and potential donors, and reviewing letters of inquiry and grant applications.

Planned Giving

Death is a subject most people avoid as sedulously as they do discussions of favorite colonoscopies or a neighbor's drywall project. But the end comes for us all, and though we might fear the Reaper we had best anticipate his eventual arrival.

Planned giving is a serviceable euphemism for what we're really talking about: estate gifts of all kinds—and there are many—but primarily getting people to remember your nonprofit in their wills. Although this can be tricky to talk about in face-to-face meetings, since the underlying subject is the death of your interlocutor, it needn't be distasteful or manipulative. Americans nearing retirement or old age have dramatically more money than that demographic has had at any time before. They can't take it with them, as all but the churls and misers understand. It has to go somewhere. Why not to your worthy cause?

Anyone over the age of 60 has probably thought about his or her mortality. They've divvied up their assets, at least in their mind, and, if they are wise, in their will. They've also pondered their legacy. That's a good word, *legacy*: Use it. Legacy speaks to the ethereal, the transcendent. It elevates a conversation about wills above the awkward question of who gets what when the subject dies. It's not about money, or the scramble therefor; it's about *legacy*.

Planned giving is preposterously underpursued. In our most recent survey, groups with annual revenue of less than $3 million realized, on average, only about two planned gifts in the preceding year. That's a shame, given that the average size of a planned gift in our survey was $135,328. (That equals a heckuva lot of $75 donations.) But what's more of a shame is that simply having a planned-giving program leads, miraculously, to planned gifts! Consider those groups with annual revenue of $3 million–$9.99 million. Those *with* a planned-giving program received an average of 34 planned gifts in the previous year, and those without, just three.

So having a planned-giving program is important. Having a planned-giving program that is central to the life of your organization—that is, something that you actively promote and encourage, rather than being just a page on a website—is even more important. In the same survey, groups that had organizationally important planned-giving programs received an average of 46 planned gifts the previous year versus an average of four for those lacking such a program. The groups in the former category reported an average of a whopping 180 pending planned gifts, compared to just six for those in the latter category. As you might imagine, the differences in planned-giving revenue between groups in these two categories is mammoth: nearly $7 million versus $1 million over the preceding five years.

We are heretics (surprise!) on the question of planned giving. Conventional wisdom has it that you need detailed information on your website and in your letters about the legal and tax implications of planned giving.

We beg—actually, we demand—to differ. The eyes glaze over at the arcana of estate law. No one wants to read that. It bogs the reader down in the mire. He or she will just set it aside for another day, which is to say the Twelfth of Never. Besides, if someone is thinking seriously about his will, he's going to deal with his own lawyer or financial planner.

For a lot of money, you can put in place a highly sophisticated planned-giving program. Or, you can put in place a highly effective one on the cheap. To do so, we recommend a three-step process:

1) *Tell people that you accept planned gifts.* This should be expressed in plain language on your website and in planned-gift letters to donors. Don't use jargon or circumlocution. Don't even use the word *bequest*. Say that if you'd like more information about leaving a gift to XYZ in your will, please contact so-and-so at such-and-such a phone number or email address. You might also include a box on reply cards that recipients can check if they'd like to learn more.

Frequency, longevity, and amount of donations determine whom to solicit, with amount being the least important of those three factors. Anyone who has given for at least five years should receive a planned-gift ask, as should those who have given significant amounts over a shorter duration.

A planned-gift letter should—*must*—be personal. If possible, include an introduction or "lift note" from someone who is leaving your organization a gift in her will. This can be a brief testimonial about why she is remembering you in her estate. The president or director of your organization should sign the main letter, which as a rule will be shorter than the typical piece of direct mail. It must be mission-centric. Emphasize the good work that a legator's gift can do after he has passed out of this world. Do not sound a transactional note in the letter. Don't write about tax benefits or the financial implications of a planned gift. That's the financial planner's job. You want to deepen the emotional bond between the letter's recipient and your group; money talk militates against that. (Though you can remind people that they can name your nonprofit as a beneficiary of a brokerage account or life insurance policy as well as a will.)

A planned-gift letter should be sent once a year. More frequent letters are unseemly and smack of cupidity or mercenary motives: "Hey, these guys are awfully anxious for me to kick off!" Less frequent letters run the risk of losing likely prospects. Again, make it personal. Avoid the generic or boilerplate at all costs. Give the name of the development officer you're asking them to contact; include a picture of the person if possible (unless he bears an unsettling resemblance to the Grim Reaper). No one wants to imagine dying alone, or among strangers, in a sterile impersonal setting. Your planned-gift request will, inevitably, provoke thoughts of death on the part of the solicitee. Remind him or her that your organization is made up of real people, of friends, comrades, teammates, who will in their daily labors honor and remember those who are kind enough to leave a bequest.

To take an example from an exemplary fundraising operation, Hillsdale College includes in its mailings a simple message surrounding a photo of an avaricious-looking Uncle Sam grasping (your!) tax dollars. It reads:

> Who Is the Beneficiary of Your Estate? Your Family and Charitable Organizations Such as Hillsdale College? Or Uncle Sam?

The simple rectangular sheet goes on to say:

> Without a will and proper estate planning, the majority of your assets may be used to fund wasteful and unconstitutional government programs. Make sure that your assets are used to support your principles. To receive a free will and estate planning guide, or for more information, please contact our Gift & Estate Planning Office.

It then provides a phone number, email address, and a web address. And that's it—nothing complicated, nothing recondite, nothing intimidating to non-lawyers, just a rather modest request that the reader think about leaving a portion of her estate to Hillsdale College.

And you know what? It works. According to the Council for Aid in Education, Hillsdale, a small liberal arts college in Michigan with a well-cultivated reputation for political conservatism, was one of only two schools to raise more money than it spent in 2015. Hillsdale raised 135.7 percent of the amount it expended in FY 2015, second only to the experimental Deep Springs College in the California desert at 144 percent. Most schools of higher education were closer to 10 percent, and even Stanford (35%) and Harvard (26%), with admittedly far higher budgets, were left in the dust by Hillsdale's incredible fundraising machine.[1]

You needn't be as pithily terse as Hillsdale. The Goldwater Institute, the Phoenix-based libertarian-conservative think-tank, mails a more substantial package to those it invites to join the Barry Goldwater Legacy Society.

The Goldwater planned-giving ask leads with a single-page lift note from a couple who made a bequest to the Goldwater Legacy Society in memory of the husband's brother, a well-known Phoenix attorney. The note, on handsome azure $7\frac{1}{4}''$ by $10\frac{1}{2}''$ letterhead stationery emblazoned with the first letter of the couple's surname, pays tribute to the deceased brother without lapsing into mawkishness. It does not feel manipulative (nor is it manipulative). It explains to recipients that the best way this couple found to honor their beloved brother and brother-in-law was through a gift that will perpetuate the ideals he held sacred, and to which he had dedicated his life. The note ends with a plea to read the enclosed letter from the Goldwater Institute's president. The signatures of the husband and wife are reproduced after the signoff.

The enclosed four-page letter is printed on heavy cream stock, signed by the Goldwater Institute president, and includes a color photo of the president next to the salutation. It refers back to the lift note, waxes autobiographical to a greater extent than most prospecting or house-file letters, and while it mentions a few of the Goldwater Institute's manifold accomplishments, it does not dwell thereon. Rather, the president discusses the importance of leaving a legacy, not only materially but as a symbolic act of faith and hope.

Goldwater does not mention the tax advantages of planned giving; instead, it invites the recipient to contact the Institute's Director of Foundation Relations and Coordinator of Planned Giving. It provides his direct phone line and email as well as the website address at which one might learn about the Barry Goldwater Legacy Society in greater detail. A response form is also included for those who have already made provision for the Society in their wills. The postage-paid business reply mail envelope is addressed to the President, and not just to the Goldwater Institute.

Finally, the Goldwater package contains an attractive 18-page booklet, chock-full of photographs, profiling several couples and individuals who have made sizeable donations to the Goldwater Institute, whether via direct cash gifts, wills or bequests, charitable trusts, gift annuities, or the transfer of IRA assets. In each case the financial details are woven, briefly, into a tale of why the benefactor or benefactress came to endow the Goldwater Institute. On the brochure's cover is a photo of a prosperous-looking white-haired gent over whose manly shoulders is draped a little boy, presumably a grandson or great-grandson. The distinguished codger doesn't look ready to kick off just yet, but he's certainly old enough to give the matter some thought.

First Things, the journal of religion and public life, also has a planned-giving club. No, it's not called *Last Things*, but rather the Richard John Neuhaus Society, after the publication's founder. On a single sheet bearing an inserted image of Father Neuhaus, crucifix in the background, *First Things*'s editor introduces the Society and deftly explains why a planned gift places the giver in the tradition of the founder: "To join the Richard John Neuhaus Society, you need only do what he did: Remember the Institute on Religion and Public Life in your estate plans. These gifts cost you nothing during your lifetime. But they will play a very important role in shaping our future." The letter closes with an invitation to make a bequest, noting that one should talk with a "trusted financial advisor or attorney" before doing so.

2) *Recognize existing planned givers.* The rare wealthy recluse may have a passion for anonymity, but most people like to have their good deeds and generosity acknowledged, at least in a dignified and understated way. You might recognize planned givers in some special fashion, or perhaps just by automatically placing them in the top level of your existing donor club while letting others know that arranging a planned gift will elevate them, too, into the donorial stratosphere.

The Freedom Foundation, a think-tank in Washington State, maintains a "Wall of Honor" on which those who pledge planned gifts are thanked for "helping to ensure that the message of freedom and liberty will continue for the next generation." It makes a somewhat more politically charged pitch for planned giving than do other organizations, though one that is consonant with its supporters' libertarian leanings:

> Each one of us already has an estate plan. It's a plan by default, a government plan.
>
> Government doesn't know or care who we were; our achievements, our faith, principles, ethics, or our devotion to our family.
>
> In this plan, hard-earned assets can be unnecessarily taxed and heirs can be left with little or nothing.

The taxman—a figure of scorn from the Bible to the Beatles—is no one's idea of a worthy legatee.

3) *Project and embody stability.* Which is to say: Get older! Planned giving is paradoxical in that discussion thereof suggests mortality but also stability. The giver will pass on but the recipient of her gift will endure. The good works flowing from the gift will benefit generations to come.

This is yet another reason to avoid The-Sky-Is-Falling fundraising. No one is going to bequeath anything to a moribund organization. "Send money or we'll close up shop!" may guilt a small number of people into making one-time donations, but a person is not going to leave you a piece of her estate if she thinks you're going to shutter your doors soon after she is in the ground.

Planned giving is not likely to prove as fruitful for newer organizations without established donor bases. It's still worth a shot, but don't be dismayed if you meet resistance. Time, in this case, will eventually come to your rescue.

Planned gifts are the pleasantest of development surprises, but they'll only happen if you lay the groundwork. Case in point: Seven or eight years ago, one of our longtime clients—let's call it the H2O Society—acquired a new donor through its direct-mail prospecting program. We'll call her Jane. Properly cultivated—that is, cultivated the AmPhil Way—Jane eventually became a major donor to H2O, giving between $10,000 and $20,000 per year.

Last summer, at our urging, and with our coordination and drafting of the letters, the H2O Society sent out a planned-giving letter to its house file. A few months later, Jane contacted them. "Your letter reminded me to put the Society in my will," she said. Shortly thereafter Jane died. She left $1 million to the H2O Society.

Jane's was not the only response to that planned-giving letter. So far it has brought in about $1.1 million—and the Lord only knows how many more estates will make provision for H2O. All this resulted from a series of three coordinated actions: (1) a direct-mail letter; (2) cultivation; and (3) a planned-giving letter.

We estimate that $1.1 million is enough to offset the net cost of H2O's entire direct-mail program for the last 12 years, with all the planned-giving letters they have sent during that time thrown in, too. Every other donor or planned gift that has come in or will come in is pure gravy, less the rather minor costs of cultivation. That adds up to millions of dollars in pure profit.

The largest planned gifts sometimes come right out of left field. Another client of ours, a nonprofit that publishes a prestigious magazine of very modest circulation, numbered among its smallest contributors a gentleman who was giving a grand total of $5 per month. That's $5, not $50 or $500. Nevertheless, he, like all donors of whatever level, received a letter advising him of the existence of the magazine's planned-giving program and its affiliated Edmund Burke Society. Apprised of its existence, he altered his will to leave the Society one-quarter of his estate. Upon his recent death that quarter translated into a bequest of $200,000.

From small things, as the bard of Asbury Park, New Jersey, once sang, big things one day come.

ENDNOTE

1. Jillian Berman, "These Tiny Colleges Trounce Stanford and Harvard in This Category," *MarketWatch*, January 27, 2016, https://www.marketwatch.com/story/these-tiny-colleges-trounce-stanford-and-harvard-in-this-category-2016-01-27.

Chapter 7

Assessing the Donor Party—and, Foundations Are People, Too!

"Donor research" is a hot niche business these days, rather as cupcake boutiques were yesterday, mac-and-cheese eateries are today, and—what?—steamed broccoli bars or donkey-cheese shoppes will be tomorrow.

How do you identify promising donors?

In general, our least favorite means is to pay a vendor a huge fee—there's always a huge fee—to examine your entire donor base and disgorge reams of data about the net worth, "giving capacity," and "propensity to give," among a thousand other measures, of the persons therein. These services will tell you who's a millionaire, who's a billionaire, who's a pauper, and who's a prince. Their computers comb through such public records as SEC (Securities and Exchange Commission) transactions and cough up the names of the wealthiest people on your list. They can more or less point you to the high-net-worth people, correlate giving capacity with age, and direct you to the best planned-giving prospects.

It sounds, in the parlance of the huckster, like a no-brainer. If you know who's got the money, this whole fundraising thing gets a lot easier, no?

Well, yes and no; if you have a donor base of perhaps 12,000 names, you'll be spending at least $3,000 on this search—not chickenfeed. Yes, you will have a universe of intelligence. But so what? You need *actionable* intelligence. A person's net worth ultimately has surprisingly little bearing on how much money he or she will give your nonprofit.

Blanket (and very expensive) research is often not terribly useful. Donor intelligence is only as meaningful as your ability to make it operational. Endless printouts of donor giving-capacity data are only nominally useful unless you have in place a system for cultivating and moving your donors up the giving ladder. Discovering that a donor is capable of contributing far more than he currently is will not in itself lead to a larger gift. You still need to cultivate that donor: to bring him or her into the life of your organization, to make him feel like a partner in some great enterprise, a friend, a compadre, a cherished benefactor. Just because a prospect is rich doesn't mean she's going to hand over a slice of her fortune to your group.

What does meaningful donor research look like? Whom should you research? Why should you research? Where do you research?

We're glad you asked.

Whom Should You Research?

The person most likely to give you a gift is the one who just gave you a gift! This is axiomatic if somewhat counterintuitive. Yes, the person has demonstrated, in the most bottom-line fashion, an affinity with your organization, but, well, he or she just gave. Shouldn't we broaden our gaze?

Not at first. Meaningful donor research begins with donors who are already giving to you. Start with your own database. At this stage, it's very simple. Three basic queries will get you started:

- ◆ Which donors have made the greatest contributions?
- ◆ Which donors have been giving the longest?
- ◆ Which donors give the most frequently?

Concentrating on these three donor subsets—greatest givers, longest givers, and most frequent givers—is the best way to start making good use of your data. Depending on the size of your house-file list, these donors should constitute the cream of your major prospects. They are, at least, folks who merit special attention. If your file has 1,000 donors, the top 100 in each category—size, longevity, frequency—should be singled out for further research.

So your first step is to search your database to sort out donors by *longevity of giving*. Not who is the oldest, or the richest, or the descendant of robber barons or Eurotrash royalty, or even who gives the most (though that is useful information, too), but who has given for the longest time. This is the best indicator of a potential major donor as well as a planned-giving prospect.

The second and companion query to run is to ask who gives with the most frequency. If someone has been giving $100 four times a year for 10 years, you've got a major and planned giving donor on your hands, if he's properly cultivated. You need to know who these people are. In too many nonprofits, especially larger ones, the metronomically regular $100 donors fall through the cracks. Maybe they get a computerized thank-you for each gift, but they never hear from the president or even a development officer. They're forgotten. This is a *huge* mistake.

Longevity and frequency speak to habits of giving, habits of commitment. Yes, other measures are, to a lesser degree, significant—you can't ignore highest past contribution—but length and frequency are the keys. When you find donors who fit the profile, build those relationships.

A talented and respected fundraiser with years of experience recently attended one of our training seminars. We know what you're thinking: This is the setup for some obnoxious horn-tooting or vulgar braggadocio, or a frat-boyish "AMPHIL RULES!" chant.

Well, this story does reflect well on us, but we'll keep it modest. The man in question is now raising funds for a historic property associated with an ex-president. He dashed off this note to us:

> Just wanted to provide you with a quick follow-up to illustrate how your advice at the West Chester, PA, seminar can be very valuable.
>
> We have been looking at the three-part select you recommended: HPC [highest past contribution], Frequency, Longevity.

A name that came up on that select just gave an unsolicited 100× previous high ($1,000 to $100,000).

Anecdotal, but enough verification for me to make sure we are doing more and more with the folks on our list who rate high in all three of these areas.

And yes, we have uncovered lots of supporters not previously on our radar thanks to this select.

Thanks again!

It's common sense, really. Organizations should use this screening method to find their top prospects among those who are already giving. Those who give frequently, have been giving for a long time, and who have given significant sums are good prospects for larger gifts. One would think this would be a *"Duh"*-quality truism within the world of professional fundraising—but it's not. Most organizations don't bother to winnow and sift their donor lists in this way. Rather, they pay WealthEngine (which "predicts who are your best buyers, donors or investors and gives you the insights you need to understand what drives their decisions") or Raiser's Edge ("a comprehensive system that helps nonprofits achieve their mission by getting the very most out of their existing fundraising strategies") to supply reams of expensive demographic research and eye-glazing data that they'll never use.

Jeremy is a Bill James disciple. He loved *Moneyball*. But James and Billy Beane and Theo Epstein and other numerate revolutionaries who have given baseball lifers a crash course in advanced statistics know that numbers are a tool, not a master. And some numbers, like pitchers' wins, just don't tell you much. (If you don't believe us, ask Denny McLain.)

Don't waste your time researching prospects who have never given you a dime if you don't first have a real understanding of those who are already giving to you. Start with the easy stuff. You acquired these donors at great cost and great effort. Cultivate them; get to know them. Researching your own stable is essential to realizing the full value of your acquisition program.

How Should You Research?

Basic donor research should help you understand whether the donor or donor prospect is a good match with your organization. Sure, just as in the realm of love, opposites can attract, but love is inscrutable and mysterious; fundraising isn't. By and large, atheists don't give to religious charities (and vice versa), conservatives don't give to liberal nonprofits (and vice versa), and those whose pet cause is encouraging the children of Jacksonville, Florida, to study engineering don't give to poetry foundations in the Pacific Northwest.

You need to discover what a donor's or a prospect's interests are, what organizations they typically support, and their previous patterns of philanthropy. These are more important than raw numbers about giving capacity. Just because a person has money doesn't mean he's going to let you have a chunk of it. Take the time to understand what a donor or prospect is trying to achieve through his giving. Is your organization a good fit? Is it a likely recipient? Don't waste time trying to sell yourself to someone who's not interested. There are plenty of prospects who *will* be interested. Your job is to find them.

There are both free and subscription databases that may help you determine whether a donor or prospect is a good fit:

- ◆ DonorSearch
- ◆ Google
- ◆ Zillow
- ◆ Anywho.com or whitepages.com
- ◆ Foundation Directory, Foundation Search, GuideStar (to access 990s with foundation giving)

- iWave
- WealthEngine (you don't *have* to have them screen your entire file)

Thorough research is the first step in soliciting major donor and foundation prospects, and it can be a useful way to begin the cultivation process. You only get one chance to make a first impression, and though no law or even custom forbids you from multiple supplications, a blind approach is almost always a mistake. It is far better to collect and synthesize information on the individual or foundation in question. Focus your research on:

- **Giving capacity, assets, and annual giving**
  Many databases will give you a giving capacity estimate. These can be useful, in a rough-and-ready if not precisely tailored sort of way. You will get a much clearer picture if you examine the donor's prior gifts to other organizations.
- **Areas of interest**
  These can be discerned by noting board participation in other organizations, giving histories, donor clubs, and professional biographies. Social media sites such as Facebook and LinkedIn often provide revealing glimpses into someone's philanthropic tendencies and personal preferences. Don't feel voyeuristic about this: You're not stalking; you're doing research!
- **Giving history**
  You know how sometimes a man will say, for public consumption, that his hobbies are playing the cello, reading Imagist poetry, and ballroom dancing, yet if you walk in on him unannounced he'll be sprawled on the La-Z-Boy stuffing his face with Cheetos and watching

pro wrestling on TV? Well, the charitable can be like that. No, they're not slobs posing as snobs; rather, there can be a sizeable gap between a foundation's or a donor's stated area of interest and their actual giving history. Their website may say one thing—we support childhood education, for example—yet their history may reveal another thing: say, numerous gifts for scholarships at universities. So take the mission statement with a grain of salt (and, given the soporific nature of most mission statements, with a strong stimulant). Just as in the eyes abides the heart, as Stephen Foster wrote, so does the pattern of giving indicate where the giver's real interests lie.

- **Religious commitments or lack thereof**
  If at all possible, discover a prospect's religious affiliation. Not only will this save you from embarrassing faux pas—bringing a Catholic a juicy hamburger on a Lenten Friday, suggesting to a Mormon that the two of you repair to the local tavern for a beer, offering to share your bag of pork rinds with an Orthodox Jew— but, more realistically, it can help you frame your proposal, meeting, or ask. This is especially true of nonprofits seeking support for missions or other faith-based initiatives.

- **Political orientation**
  Political orientation can offer powerful (though hardly failsafe) clues to a prospect's philanthropic bent. Certainly it is determinative when the nonprofit has a distinctive ideological coloration, though in other cases a donor's preference for Democratic or Republican (or Green or Libertarian) candidates indicates little or nothing about his receptivity to a pitch from the symphony orchestra or a private school. Public disclosure

filings, available online or through most major donor research databases, will list a prospect's past political contributions if they have been large enough.

◆ **History of the foundation or individual—how it/ he/she got its/his/her money**

Whence the dough? Was it inherited? Did great-grandfather strike oil? Manufacture dice? Bootleg during Prohibition? Is the prospect or donor a self-made man who pulled himself up by the bootstraps? Or did he marry the heiress to a sewing-machine fortune? Is the foundation endowed by a woman who founded a cosmetics company? Is she the author of Ayn Rand–inflected *Looking Out for #1* bestsellers?

For both individuals and foundations, knowing the source of charitable wealth can assist in the cultivation and proposal processes. It provides a window into the interests of the giver and suggests possible avenues of approach. If nothing else it strengthens your conversational arsenal in face-to-face meetings. Woe betide the nonprofit executive who discourses on the virtue of altruism in making his pitch to the Randian (who, come to think of it, is an improbable candidate for giving, anyway) or who jokes about his ineptness with computers in a meeting with a Silicon Valley 30-something billionaire.

◆ **Geographic focus of giving, and geographic location of the foundation or individual**

Place matters. At least it does to some people. Many foundations and individuals have a geographic focus to their giving: Newark, New England, Texas border towns, Provo, the South, Greenwich Village, the Rocky Mountains—every nook and cranny and neighborhood and region of this diverse country. If your location matches the stated area of concentration, marvelous: You have a homeboy's in. But even if there is a, shall we say, geographic disjunction between your headquarters in Baltimore and a foundation's assertion of Oregon pride, explore a bit further before crossing it off the list. Not infrequently do foundations, especially, record a giving history that is at odds with their stated focus.

◆ **Largest grantees, especially recently**
Upon whom has the prospect or donor, whether foundation or individual, lavished its largest gifts of late? How long has that grantee been a recipient of the largesse? Did the giving increase over time? At what level did it start? Did it rise incrementally or all at once? This information offers clues as to the level of your ask and the probability of success.

◆ **Typical range of grants, in size**
There is no sense in asking for a $100,000 gift from an organization or individual that has never made a gift over $10,000. Knowing typical grant sizes will assist you in crafting a realistic proposal. We are put in mind of a nonprofit executive who, upon learning that one of the names on the donor list belonged to a well-known Hollywood director, hustled out to Beverly Hills for a meeting. Though the director's previous gifts to the nonprofit had been modest in size, the executive, assuming that money grows on palm trees and that anyone whose name is boldly emblazoned on a movie poster is fantastically wealthy, asked for $100,000. The director, nonplussed, snorted in disbelief. The lunch concluded amiably enough but no gift was ever forthcoming. Know thy donor!

◆ **Typical number of grantees in recent years**
Knowing how many organizations a donor or foundation has supported in recent years is a good clue to its robustness. Has the number waxed, waned, or remained constant? Study the pattern.

- **Approaches**

  Does the foundation have a stated policy on accepting unsolicited proposals? Is it known to respond to letters of inquiry or meeting requests? Even if the answer to the latter question is no, a succinct and polite letter of inquiry (LOI) or request for a meeting is not misplaced. Nothing ventured, nothing gained.

- **Is the foundation professionally staffed?**

  The answer to this will help determine your avenue of approach. If the organization is professionally staffed, it is probably not a good idea (unless you have a close personal tie) to seek a meeting first with a board member, especially if there are clearly articulated approach guidelines. You don't want to bruise any egos or hurt any feelings. No one likes to be bypassed. Go through the established channels. If a foundation has no staff, your approach strategy would typically be similar to that for a major individual donor or prospect.

- **Miscellaneous information, including personal and foundation histories**

  Look for any edge, any scrap of information that gives you a sense of the character of the person or the foundation. It can be family history, civic involvements, offbeat enthusiasms, or idiosyncrasies. You can advert to these, with appropriate subtlety, in personal meetings or conversations or, if the opportunity presents itself, in the proposal itself.

We Pause for This Brief Statistical Message

In our American Philanthropic surveys, foundation grants accounted for a surprisingly high percentage of revenue: While nationwide, foundation grants are the source of about one in every five charitable dollars, they supplied an average of approximately one-third of the development revenue to the groups in our samples.

At the risk of causing your eyes to glaze over, here are a few other numerical takeaways from our survey:

◆ "Highly effective" organizations received an average of 41.6 foundation grants annually while the others averaged 21.3 grants.
◆ The mean number of foundation proposals and letters of inquiry submitted per year was 31.8, with the tiers breaking down as such: for organizations with revenue of $100–$499K: 18.7; $500K–$999K: 18.1; $1M–$2.99M: 33.6; $3M–$9.99M: 42.2; and $10M+: 107.8.
◆ Large organizations get more grants and larger grants than smaller organizations. Grants received, and average size thereof, broke down as follows: $100K–$499K: 6.3 and $16,274; $500K–$999K: 9.6 and $24,536; $1M–$2.99M: 30.5 and $21,544; $3M–$9.99M: 32.0 and $40,803; and $10M+: 73.4 and $84,570.

Okay, so the bigger you are the more money you can ask for and the more money you can get. The rich get richer, as the eternal plaint goes.[1]

Foundation Solicitations

You've done the research. You've filled in the background. You have an ambitious yet plausible list of foundations that might be responsive to your entreaties.

Now you need a strategy. It needn't be perfect; it doesn't have to rely upon a rare alignment of the planets. People get too hung up on the ideal, waiting for that moment that just doesn't come, and before you know it two years have gone by and you've nothing to show for it. So move with deliberate speed.

First, the entree, and we don't mean Beef Wellington: This is one instance where a friend of a friend can be useful. Make it hard for the foundation staff to ignore you. If you, one of your staffers, or a board member knows someone at the foundation, by all means use that connection. Request a personal meeting with the apposite foundation staffer, even if you lack an intercessor. Will you get a meeting upon every request? No. Should you be depressed by this? No way! We're going where there's no depression, as the Carter Family exhorts. For every 10 meeting requests you may get only one or two meetings. That's okay. Keep trying.

There are over 75,000 private foundations in America. They donate well over $40 billion annually. Don't wait for an introduction. Go out and contact them.

Here's another example of how we are different from the mob of credentialed fundraising professionals. In applying for grants from foundations, it is standard operating procedure among many fundraising professionals—especially in large institutions like hospitals, universities, and national public charities—never to approach a foundation unless you are invited, have a strong connection through a board member, or have some other inside track. For instance, one of your board members takes one of their board members to lunch, thus setting in motion a chain of events that leads to a sizeable grant. Such personal ties can be valuable and should be exploited when possible, but contrary to the world-weary adage, it's not *always* who you know.

Some institutional fundraisers wait years before actually applying to a foundation that may be likely to fund them. They wait until they have some solid connection to the foundation. We see this over and over again with our academic clients. Their best practice is to wait until they have a likely "yes."

Don't let the perfect be the enemy of the good. This approach betrays a naïve understanding of how foundation decision-making processes actually work. We have found a great deal of success—in fact, we are consistently surprised at how successful we have been—by *not* following industry best practices in foundation relations. Research a bunch of foundations that give to like causes, put your best foot forward, and dive in. It works surprisingly well.

Again, practical wisdom should prevail in fundraising, not industry best practices. Do what works. If you find another approach that is shown to be more effective, then adapt.

Your foundation research will pay off in that you'll be able to spread your net widely but also wisely. Approach any that give off a glimmer of promise—even if their websites discourage unsolicited requests or instruct grant-seekers to wait for an invitation before submitting an application. The way to get an invitation is by asking for one. Get your metaphorical foot in the door. Be persistent—not obnoxious, but persistent.

Your meeting request letter, especially if you're coming in cold, should be concise yet informative. Get right to the point: Ask for a meeting in the first paragraph. Give a specific date range. Don't say "anytime over the next year" and don't say "9:30 a.m. on November 15." Say something like "I'll be in Washington the week of April 10–14 and would be grateful for the chance to meet with you."

Keep the letter to a single page, if you can. Never go longer than a page and a half; lengthy introductory letters carry the not-so-faint whiff of crackpottery. If the recipient is unfamiliar with your organization, give her a slightly expanded version of your elevator pitch. Don't send DVDs or thumb drives advertising your group's work; don't send anything that requires a box or unusually shaped envelope. (You may, however, send an annual report or prospectus.)

Don't get hung up on securing a meeting. If a foundation is not responsive or you can't get to Fargo or Duluth for a face-to-face, then send a letter of inquiry. Don't just use a boilerplate letter with a change of name; customize it. Of course you're working from a template, but you want this to grab them, not make them yawn with its generic blandness. You might begin, "I am writing to ask for your permission to submit a proposal to the Smith Foundation. Given your support for [Allied Cause] and [Allied Cause] I think we may have common interests. Our founder Jones has been associated with you in the past." Or: "Our bishop Thomas O'Hara suggested that I contact you." Drop those names. It's always possible they'll fall with a thud to the ground, but proper names, especially recognizable ones, cause readers to look twice.

The ideal LOI is somewhat longer than a meeting request letter: Think two pages. Explain who you are, what you have done in the past, and what you want. There are different schools of thought as to the mention of money. If it won't scare them—"We would respectfully request a grant of $15,000 to strengthen our childhood literacy program"—then by all means suggest a number. If it's $150,000, though, or $1.5 million, you might want to hold off until your next exchange.

Now comes the hard part: the follow-up. It's unlikely that a foundation program officer will call you the day he receives your letter and beg you to make a formal application. It would be nice, but it's not going to happen. You have to follow up on your initial contact. As in the case of those meeting request letters we discussed earlier, a letter is really just an excuse to call later.

Phone or email the program officer. This greatly increases your odds of getting a chance at bat. How many follow-ups are too many? If you're calling cold, two tries is probably sufficient. If you have a link to the foundation or the officer, however thin, be more persistent.

Okay, let's say you get the green light: "We have received your LOI and would be happy to consider your proposal." What next?

1) *Include a strong cover letter and executive summary.* Most foundations are overwhelmed with proposals: Entities in the business of giving away money usually are. Many smaller foundations, especially family foundations, have no dedicated staff to wade through them, winnowing the deserving from the dross. Unless you have been invited to apply, the foundation representative who reviews your proposal is probably looking for reasons to reject it. Nothing personal· just innate human laziness.

Don't give him a reason to toss your application into the recycle bin. Use your cover letter and executive summary to make a strong, concise case for support. Keep the padding and the public-relations lingo to an absolute minimum: Explain, with admirable succinctness, what your nonprofit does and what you would do with the monies requested.

Oftentimes, the people who ultimately make the funding decisions—members of the foundation's board—don't see your full proposal. Rather, they receive a summary prepared by the staff, which is combined with other request summaries into a board book. Your cover letter and executive summary are likely to be included in this board book. Make them count.

2) *Give context for your request.* Many proposals dive straight into the nuts and bolts (ouch! that would hurt) without first answering the critical questions: "Why are we doing this? Why should you care?" Step back and set the scene. What's the problem you're addressing? Why is it important? How is your organization well-suited to addressing said problem? If there are other organizations engaged in similar work, how is yours different? (Do not, of course, trash the competition. That's bad form.)

If you're not sure you've answered these questions well, give the proposal to someone you respect who is outside of your organization and relatively unfamiliar with your work. Does it make sense to her? Is it compelling? Get candid feedback and modify accordingly.

3) *Customize the request to the foundation's requirements.* Read closely the guidelines, which will be posted online or enclosed with the foundation's letter inviting application. Do not exceed the recommended (or required) length! Doing your own thing annoys the heck out of foundation staffers and gets you off on the wrong foot. At American Philanthropic, we use the bowdlerized acronym *ATFQ*: Answer the Frickin' Question! Despite what partisans of free-spirited child-centric education say, coloring outside the lines is *not* always a good idea. And verbosity can be a real turn-off.

Without grandstanding, show them that you've done your homework. Link your mission to theirs; make it seem a natural fit.

4) *Pass the straight-face test.* It's okay to accentuate the positive, to give your proposal the best possible spin, but don't just make things up. And don't include everything but the kitchen sink in your budget; staffers and board members don't want to feel as if they're being played. On the flipside, don't shoot yourself in the foot by dramatically underestimating the time and budget needed to execute your project. You needn't get overly detailed ($24 for parking...) but don't fail to include salaries and overhead: It doesn't happen without electricity!

Be confident but retain a sense of humility. After all, if you receive the grant you'll probably have to report back on how well you've done and how you spent the money, so set achievable, realistic goals that won't leave you looking like an out-of-his-depth naif or a mendacious fool.

5) *Pay attention to details.* Leo Tolstoy never wrote a grant proposal, nor did Mark Twain. Your own prose may be infused with Tolstoyan sweep or Twainian wit, but your proposal is unlikely to be a literary masterpiece. The genre is just too constraining. Nevertheless, you need prose that is more than serviceable, and if your talents don't lie in that direction, consider outsourcing composition to someone who writes well.

Proofread your materials before submission. Typos, to borrow NASA flight director Gene Kranz's mantra in *Apollo 13*, are not an option. Spell everything correctly, including proper names. (You wouldn't believe how often supplicants misspell a funder's or foundation's name. They may as well have just scrawled BURN BEFORE READING atop the application.)

Pay attention to the visual, too. The design of your proposal should convey a sense of competence and professionalism, highlighting the content and making it easy to skim and digest. It should look like a business proposal. Don't go overboard; you're shooting for polished, not slick. Use headers, bullets, and other cues to differentiate sections. Use legible, grownup font. (Skip the comic sans in 8 point and go for Times New Roman or Garamond 12.5.) Include a list of all requested attachments—and actually attach them. These will likely include your annual report, your 990, and your audited financials. Brief biographies of your leadership and board members are also helpful (no refrigerator magnets, though).

Don't get hung up on crafting the perfect proposal or the perfect letter of inquiry. Don't just dash it off; in the matter of foundation proposals, the late poet Allen Ginsberg's dictum "first thought, best thought" may not be the ideal strategy. Your inner editor will keep whispering in your ear, "Emend! Emend! Emend!" and that's all well and good, for a day or a week, but eventually you have to shut that damned nuisance up and send out the proposal. As another poet, this one from Meridian, Mississippi, once sang, you cannot win if you do not play.

6) *Remember that foundations are run by people.* They're not staffed by ghosts in a machine or artificial intelligence clones. They're run by living, breathing men and women, whether professional staff, family members, or the donors themselves. Remember this as you approach them. As with any relationship, you want to be polite, to listen, to be honest, to be sensitive to their likes and dislikes, and to show appreciation and not take their kindnesses for granted.

So communicate effectively. Ask questions if you're confused. Say thank you if they give you a grant. Don't talk to them only when you want something; let them occasionally see you in a pose other than hat-in-hand. Take note of deadlines and be timely. If something goes awry on a project, don't wait until your report is due to say that things didn't work out; contact the funder and figure out an alternative path forward.

We can't say this too often: *Foundations are people, too.*

Anthropomorphizing philanthropic bureaucracies is a bit weird, but foundations are staffed and run by real human beings. (We have our doubts about Bill and Melinda Gates, but in keeping with our subject we'll be charitable.) Even those that project an impersonal, hyper-rational front may turn out to be surprisingly human. Helpful staffers may talk you through an application. They may steer you toward or away from buzzwords or magic maxims.

If you've developed a relationship with a staff member, or with the principal in the case of one-person shops, you needn't go all stiff on him or her in your formal communications. Don't be slangy, but don't act as if you've never engaged, either. As with potential individual benefactors, meet face to face with foundation personnel if you can. We know of an attorney for a couple of small but well-endowed foundations who only directs money to people whose hand he has shaken and into whose eyes he has looked.

If you're way off base, or not even in the ballpark, your application will be discarded without ceremony. If, however, you look like a possibility, your submission will be placed in a folder and passed out to board members, who'll give it the thumbs up or down. This is where your crisply worded executive summary of one or two pages will be critical: It's your unmediated opportunity to directly address those charged with the disposition of your application.

Okay, let's say you've sent out 30 foundation proposals. How many checks therefrom are you likely to cash in the next six months? Probably none; this is a long game. Patience is a difficult virtue to master, but you'll need it. Typically, it takes 12 to 18 months to cultivate a new foundation. So don't get hung up on a single must-have grant. As your mother once told you, there are plenty of fish in the sea. (There are about 75,000 in this particular body of water.)

Temper your expectations and those of board members, who often think that their suggestion, "Let's get a grant!" can be accomplished with a snap of the fingers. Remember: You're not in this for the short haul, for the quick-and-easy strike. A foundation strategy takes two to three years to pay off, but when it does, many of these grants will be annuals.

Don't be thin-skinned about rejections. Even Ted Williams at the plate and George Clooney at the singles bar struck out, at least now and then. Ask why you were rejected and how you might modify your next application for support. And if you've received a grant, be sure to keep the relevant staff people in the loop. Let them know what's going on, and how you're putting that benefaction to good use. Don't be the grantee equivalent of the Christian who only shows up in church on Christmas or Easter; keep in touch with the people who constitute the foundation at times of the year other than when the application deadline rolls around.

Renew acquaintances, too. In 2014, American Philanthropic took on a client, a West Coast think-tank, that had been consistently funded by The Lynde and Harry Bradley Foundation at $50,000 per year until 2010, when, in the manner of a mystery novel, that funding simply stopped, and turnover at the think-tank was such that no one knew that Bradley had once been a regular and generous grantor, let alone why the support had ended.

We brought this hidden history to their attention. The vigorous new CEO said that he knew a Bradley board member. He called to let her know that an application was forthcoming. We asked for $100,000, which seemed to graze the upper limits of possibility without ascending into avarice. Bradley awarded $75,000, which the think-tank employed to great effect, keeping Bradley in the loop as their projects progressed. Two years later, the think-tank is the recipient of a seven-figure grant.

The moral of the story is: Don't give up on lapsed donors!

As careful and meticulous as you may be, elements of the foundation process are out of your control. Some decision makers, especially those from small or family foundations, can be downright irrational. They can be charmingly idiosyncratic or maddeningly mercurial, depending upon where you sit. On an impulse, or in response to some stray scrap of information—"I heard this on NPR"; "I saw this on *The Bachelor*"—they will ignore the ostensible mission of the foundation and direct its funds to persons or causes of questionable pertinence. And there's nothing you can do about it. So send out as many plausible proposals as you can.

No matter how formidably impersonal a front their websites present, foundations consist of people: flawed, fallible, sometimes ridiculous people.

Case in point: The foundation whose leading light was the son of its endower. The board met twice yearly to dole out its grants. The son, or sottish scion, showed up at the spring meeting drunk as a skunk. (The meeting was scheduled at 11 a.m., by the way, not 11 p.m.) He was not what you'd call a happy drunk; when in his cups this fellow became mean, truculent, hostile. He announced, in slurred speech, that every single one of the proposals before the board was garbage, and that they should be rejected summarily. Since the board customarily deferred to this dipsomaniacal dauphin, the applications were deposited in the nearest recycling bin. The meeting adjourned without a single grant having been approved.

Fast forward six months. The board gathers for its fall meeting. It has a new set of applications to consider. But there's not much considering to be done. By law, a foundation has to part with 5 percent of its giving capacity on a three-year rolling basis. And since this one had, as yet, not given away a thin dime all year due to the debacle at its spring meeting, the board was forced to approve every one of the applications at its autumn meeting.

Is there a moral to this story? Not really, though the relicts of the Woman's Christian Temperance Union might disagree. Surely this is not an example of giving from the heart, though just as certainly it is decidedly non-rational. It's capricious, and ridiculously arbitrary. Is it effective? Darned if we know.

On a loftier note, one of our good friends with extremely deep pockets endows, quite amply, a foundation. He is a wonderful man, and like many men of great wealth he has his tics and crotchets. Or perhaps it is more accurate to say that he has a well-formed personality, and it takes a while to understand and appreciate all the folds and contours of that personality.

His giving capacity is considerable. That much one can ascertain with minimal research. Yet many of his gifts are modest in size. He likes to spread the wealth a bit, and get to know people before he commits substantial sums to their operations.

He had funded various projects of a respected DC think-tank at up to $100,000 over the years, though he and the think-tank's president were hardly intimates. In fact, they barely knew each other. But the president was aware of the donor's giving capacity. The president was planning a major expansion of his think-tank, and he realized that this donor with whom he was only hazily acquainted could fund it with a single check.

So he requested an audience and flew across the country, proverbial hat in hand. The president got right to the point. He asked for a gift of $5 million—or 50 times the size of any previous gift by this donor. After all, he had the money, and an obvious affinity with the think-tank's work.

But it was a terrible ask. The jump was too large, and more crucially, the men were almost strangers to each other. You have to have a relationship before making a big ask. You need a foundation of trust, of security, of friendship. And you need to know with whom you are dealing. Some rich people, or foundation executives, enjoy being flattered or paid obsequious attention. Others don't. The wise fundraiser will know—or ascertain—the difference.

Don't get greedy. Don't ask for too much too soon. Don't kill—or scare off—the goose that might lay the golden egg.

Shortly after the $5 million flop, the philanthropist visited another think-tank he had supported, this one at a far more modest level. It was a small but feisty outfit, headquartered far from the Potomac, and with a budget that was a fraction of the war chest of most Washington, DC, think-tanks.

The philanthropist loved these guys. He felt immediately at home with them. For lunch they served him pizza on paper plates, and for the next week he raved about the frugality of this group. "Those fellas don't waste money!" he said admiringly. They had appealed to his sense of thrift and economy. Their treasury would soon be amply rewarded.

The lessons of this story are obvious. Individual donors have idiosyncrasies and quirks, like all human beings. Although "think outside the box" has become a trite and hackneyed maxim, too many fundraisers act as if men or women of means come from the same box, the same category, and will be impressed by the same pitch. So research the object of your solicitation—never walk into a meeting cold and unprepared if you can help it—but don't *over*prepare. You don't need to put on a dog-and-pony show. These can often seem like Potemkin Village tours, phony and off-putting. Be yourself. Avoid the stilted or the scripted. Get to know the person; in raising money, human relationships usually precede substantial monetary relationships.

Relationships matter. Everything you'd do to build relationships with individual donors, do with foundations. If you're sending donors a book, send one to the foundation. Make sure they get your newsletter or periodic updates, though not your house-file asks. If you're going to be in town, schedule a visit.

Foundations will test your patience. They can be slow, uncommunicative, irksome, but don't give up. Persistence will pay off, eventually.

ENDNOTE

1. On average, about 5 percent of nonprofit funding comes from corporations. Bigness likes bigness: Mean revenue from corporate gifts to the largest nonprofits in our sample ($10M+: $791,857) dwarfed the mean revenue of the smaller nonprofits, though, curiously, corporate gift revenue as a percentage of total contribution revenue was just 2 percent for these largest organizations, with the smaller tiers ranging from 8 to 12 percent.

Conclusion

Fundraising can be a frustrating endeavor. It's a job that could try the patience of Job. You won't always close the deal or make the shot. The rejections can make you feel like you're back at the high-school dance, pawing the ground with your shoes and trying to work up the nerve to approach the next boy or girl who'll turn you down.

And for those who go out on the road, it can be lonely. We like those Lucullan Red Roof Inn continental breakfasts as much as the next guy, but travel isn't all stale donuts and glamour. There are long lines at airport security. You miss your son's birthday, your daughter's dance recital, your spouse's good moods. You are mesmerized into depression by the hotel-room wallpaper. You clear out the mini-bar. The maids are starting to talk. You're as morose as a Jackson Browne song.

But as Steve Miller sang about that big old jet airliner whose ridiculously narrow legroom you curse, sometimes you've got to go through hell before you get to heaven.

The rewards for a fundraising job well done are wonderfully gratifying, not to mention remunerative. You are enriching the treasury of a good cause and the lives of so many people, from givers to recipients. You are strengthening the bonds of community; you are fortifying civil society; you are enhancing the public weal; you are, in ways both tangible and transcendent, improving the lot of real people: of your brothers and sisters, your town and your country, your world and our world.

And the occasional frustrations pale before the rewards of a fundraising job well done. The payoff is sweet; the satisfaction is good for the soul (and, less importantly but not unimportantly, the bank account).

We've warned you of the missteps and stumbles on the path ahead, but believe us, sometimes it all comes together—as it will for you, if you exercise patience and persistence and good humor.

Consider this handful of representative cases from the files of American Philanthropic:

◆ A Catholic campus outreach program undertook—and is going to successfully complete—a $15 million capital campaign. The key building block was an enormous gift from a donor whose previous contributions, while generous, had never before been enough to cause a raised eyebrow, let alone an incredulous *gulp*.

  How did the fundraiser make this happen? He was thorough and prepared. He had cultivated a relationship with this donor for years, even though the donor was not in the top tier of the organization's supporters. So he requested and got a meeting, where he proved to be an articulate and enthusiastic advocate. He knew his stuff. He presented a well-written and attractively designed capital-campaign prospectus. He left that meeting with the promise, soon redeemed, of a $2.5 million cash gift.

◆ A passionate education reformer had a dream: He wanted to start a classical boarding school in Kansas. Skeptics told him that this was pie-in-the-sky, an outlandish and unachievable fantasy. Why not build a Taj Mahal in Topeka? He'd have just as good a chance of success.

  The reformer did his homework. He created a strong case for why this school was necessary. It sounded plausible, even praiseworthy. But there was this little matter of money. His goal was to raise $5 million in the first five years. He held an open house and invited an audience of friends and well-wishers and local people whom his research had told him might share his interest in education reform. He stood up and told them about his plans, speaking from the heart but with a solid grounding underneath his feet.

A local farmer, a shy, quiet man he knew slightly, came up after his talk. The farmer had been moved. "I'll underwrite two scholarships," he said. Outstanding! The school's founder asked the farmer to stick around for the rest of the day. He did. The farmer listened thoughtfully as the founder explained his vision to other potential supporters and parents who were checking out the school as a possible landing spot for their children. One parent expressed concern that if the school fell short of the fundraising goal, it might be forced to cut corners in a way that would imperil its mission. As the open house closed, the farmer approached the founder. "Forget the two scholarships," he said. "I'll give you $250,000 a year for five years." Two nights later the founder and his wife had dinner with the farmer and his wife to discuss this wholly unexpected gift. By evening's end, the gift had risen to $400,000 a year for five years.

At this writing, the school's first building is up, and its first class begins studies in a matter of weeks.

◆ Be prepared, as the Boy Scout motto goes. Another American Philanthropic client, a small group that promotes healthy eating, asked a large Houston-based foundation with which it had no previous contact for a meeting. The well-phrased request was granted. As the fundraiser was making her travel arrangements, she received word that not only was she getting a meeting, but the foundation executive wanted a proposal on his desk within three days. With our help, the fundraising staff quickly put together a solid and convincing proposal. Why do we know it was convincing? Because within a week of the meeting, the Houston foundation had pledged a half-million-dollar grant to the advocates for healthy eating—not bad for a group whose annual budget is less than $2 million.

◆ *First Things*, the previously referenced journal of religion and public life, began notifying readers via a midyear mailing of its planned-giving club, the Richard John Neuhaus Society. When one of its long-time supporters, whose gifts had always been modest, recently died, he left *First Things* $200,000—his action spurred by that house-file letter asking readers to consider remembering the journal in their will. This example could be multiplied a hundredfold.

◆ A Washington, DC, think-tank, dismayed by middling returns from its yearend direct-mail campaigns, took our advice and lengthened its letter, asked for specific amounts, and coordinated the physical mailing with a digital campaign. The result was an 88 percent increase in revenue over its previous yearend campaign, from $133,000 to over $250,000.

The moral of these stories: *This stuff works*. Not every time, but it works over time. Absorb and apply these lessons and they will work for *you*.

When you have doubts, when the stress of the road and the frustration and rejection and everyday glitches and toe-stubbings get you down, take heart. *You will succeed.*

Sursum corda, friends!

Acknowledgments

While our names are on this book, many of the ideas, and not infrequently the words themselves, come from our dedicated colleagues at American Philanthropic. Since we founded the firm in 2009, we have been blessed to work with several dozen incredibly intelligent, hard-working men and women who love American civil society so much that, in many cases, they made the otherwise unaccountable, perhaps even irresponsible decision to jump on board with a consulting firm whose partners quite frankly admitted that most of the time they had no idea what they were doing. Our talented partners, Doug Schneider and Liz Palla, deserve special mention here, but we hereby give our hearty and heartfelt gratitude to all of our colleagues past and present. And while we're at it, allow us to thank our own and our consultants' families, especially our and their spouses, for putting up with all the travel-related absences that are the consultant's lot.

Bill Kauffman, were he blessed with a better literary agent, would have insisted on a "with" credit for this book. As it stands, he must be satisfied with a lousy acknowledgment. What wit there is in these pages is his doing, as are the 50 or so words that will have you scrambling for your online dictionaries. Despite the dated musical references he insisted on inserting into the text, since Bill is America's premier literary advocate for the localism so essential to the health of voluntary associations we are honored to have him as our collaborator.

What is valuable in this book has been ripped off—legally, of course!—from the many teachers, friends, and mentors we have met along our journeys. We don't have space to thank everyone who has contributed significantly to our thinking about fundraising, but we do want to extend special thanks to Wick Allison, Johnny Burtka, Spencer Masloff, Fred and Peggy Clark, Tom Earnshaw, Carl Helstrom III, Bill Schambra, Kristina Mitten Sanders, and the late John Von Kannon.

Finally, it will sound like a cliché but is nevertheless true that we have learned the most from our clients. The sheer amount of energy, time, and resources they are willing to invest in the work of charity is remarkable and inspiring. We are exceedingly grateful to them for letting us be part of their work—and to thus be part of what really makes America great.

About the Authors

Jeremy Beer is the co-founder of and principal partner at American Philanthropic, LLC. He took his doctorate in psychology from the University of Texas at Austin, has served as a nonprofit executive and member of various nonprofit boards, and has published on issues related to philanthropy, fundraising, politics, and culture in outlets such as the *Washington Post*, *First Things*, and the *Utne Reader*. Jeremy is the author of *The Philanthropic Revolution: An Alternative History of American Charity* as well as the forthcoming *Oscar Charleston: The Life and Legend of Baseball's Greatest Forgotten Player*. He lives in Phoenix.

Jeffrey Cain, co-founder of American Philanthropic, is now the CEO of CrossFit, Inc., the global fitness and health company. He served honorably in the US Marine Corps and holds a PhD in English Renaissance Literature. Jeff has worked as President of the Arthur N. Rupe Foundation, Secretary of the Lillian S. Wells Foundation, and Executive Vice President of the Intercollegiate Studies Institute. He is the author of *Protecting Donor Intent: How to Define and SafeGuard Your Philanthropic Principles* and has written numerous articles in a variety of publications on nonprofits, fundraising, and philanthropy. He lives in Seattle.

Index